FAITH IN THE MEDIEVAL WORLD

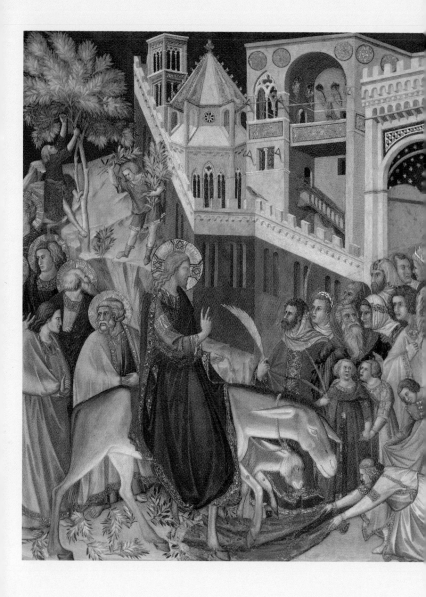

Faith in the Medieval World

G.R. Evans

A LION BOOK

The crusaders besiege
Constantinople in this
tapestry from Moldavia
monastery.

Previous pages:
Jesus riding into
Jerusalem on a donkey,
to face his crucifixion.
Fresco from *The Story
of the Passion of Christ*
by Pietro Lorenzetti.

Page one:
Christ in Majesty by
Vitale da Bologna.

Copyright © 2002 G.R. Evans
This edition copyright © 2002 Lion Publishing

The author asserts the moral right
to be identified as the author of this work

Published by
Lion Publishing plc
Mayfield House, 256 Banbury Road,
Oxford OX2 7DH, England
www.lion-publishing.co.uk
ISBN 0 7459 5101 5

First edition 2002
10 9 8 7 6 5 4 3 2 1 0

A catalogue record for this book is available
from the British Library

Typeset in 9/12 Modern 880

Printed and bound in China

Contents

Introduction

People today who are used to talk of globalism will find a 'globalism' in the smaller world of medieval Europe, too. The period known as the Middle Ages stretched for 1,000 years, from the end of the ancient world in the fourth and fifth centuries AD to the Reformation and Renaissance of the 16th century. In terms of people's values, priorities and interests, it is surprising how much stayed the same in all that time. The explanation lies in the culturally 'unifying' effect of the Christian faith.

Christianity was not a force for political unity. There has rarely been a period in Western Europe with so much war in it. In Northern Europe, the whole 'upper class' was dedicated to the profession of soldiery, with the exception of those who were church leaders. But Christianity did create a unity of fundamental ideas about the world, and of assumptions about its purpose. The result was a cultural stability remarkable in its powers to last throughout 1,000 years of social, economic and political change. The shared medieval culture went far beyond the obviously 'religious' aspects of Christianity, but it is impossible to understand that culture without first understanding something of the priorities Christianity imposed upon it.

Christians could go into a church anywhere in medieval Western Europe and find the same symbols, 'rites', or forms of worship, and the same religious language, Latin. Although the Western Church eventually stretched from the Atlantic Ocean to the borders of Greece, and from Scandinavia to the border with Islam in the south, almost everyone 'belonged' to this community and was consciously a part of it. In the Eastern half of the Roman empire, Christians worshipped in Greek, and the style of their church life was subtly different from that of worshippers in the Western half. However, the basics were the same, together with most of the symbolism in Christian art. The Christian faith of East and West was, in almost every point, identical.

This book is mainly about the medieval West, because another book in this series, *Faith in the Byzantine World*,

The cathedral of Seville dominating the skyline.

looks at faith in the East. But the Church – divided though it was by the Schism of 1054 into 'East' and 'West' – was a single community of faith throughout the medieval millennium, and some hints of the flavour of that Eastern world have a place in this book, too.

There were few people of other faiths in any part of Europe, except in southern Spain. Communities of Jews were to be met in the towns of Europe. In southern Spain, for some centuries, Islam held political control by conquest, and there Christians were in the position of 'subject people'. This is reflected in the surviving medieval architecture of Spain, where the great cathedrals tend to be of much later date than those in the north of Europe.

The World Through Medieval Eyes

In 'Christian Europe' in the Middle Ages, the 'social' expectation was that people would regard themselves as Christians. It was almost unheard of for anyone to say that he or she did not believe in God at all, and the levels of 'popular' piety were high, even if they were sometimes little more than superstition. It is important not to lose sight of that contrast between an 'educated' understanding of the faith and a more diffuse 'religiousness' in the population.

Many of the ideas and principles which make up the Christian 'faith' are abstract and sophisticated. Most of the population was illiterate. There is evidence that it clung to its old 'gods', the little pagan deities who were local and familiar, and small enough to seem like family friends, by transferring loyalty to saints. Undoubtedly, there was sometimes confusion in the popular mind, and a tendency to revere these saints as though they were deities. Nevertheless, there were certain outward signs of a society of *practising* Christians. During the Middle Ages, almost every child was christened in infancy. Almost everyone went to church regularly. Almost everyone was married in church and buried in consecrated ground.

An outlaw religion

The early Christian period is a long story of persecution and exclusion, for the first Christians tended to come from the lower social classes and were not sufficiently

'It had been my mother's custom to take cakes and bread and wine to the shrines of the saints on the saint's day of each. [Now] she learned to bring to the shrines of the martyrs a heart full of prayers which were much purer than any such gift. In this way she was able to give as much as she was able to the poor.'

AUGUSTINE,
CONFESSIONS, VI.2

'Saul kept up his violent threats of murder against the followers of the Lord... As Saul was coming near the city of Damascus, suddenly a light from the sky flashed round him. He fell to the ground and heard a voice saying to him, "Saul, Saul! Why do you persecute me?" "Who are you, Lord?" he asked. "I am Jesus, whom you persecute," the voice said. "But get up and go into the city, where you will be told what you must do."'

ACTS 9:1–6

powerful or privileged to make their faith socially acceptable. One of the most extraordinary features of the history of Christianity is the way that this 'outlaw' religion became so universally accepted in the medieval West. State approval came only in the fourth century, when the Roman emperor Constantine was 'converted' and declared himself a Christian.

Conversion in the Roman empire

We shall be looking at the 'political' consequences in chapter 6. The first thing to consider is how far the 'conversion' of the Roman empire meant that everyone had a clear understanding of the Christian faith or held it with real inner enthusiasm.

'Conversion' contains the idea of a 'turning'. This eventually came to be the word used when someone entered a monastery as an adult, because that meant a 'turning' (*conversio*) from the world to a fuller commitment to the living of a Christian life. But it was understood from the very beginning that there was another, more profound sense to conversion. Someone who had previously not believed in the God of the Christians at all, or who had held only a half-hearted belief, could suddenly become ardent in his or her convictions. The apostle Paul was first known as Saul, and he was famous for the zeal with which he persecuted the earliest Christians, whom he saw as a threat to the Jewish religion at a time when they were growing in numbers. The New Testament (Acts 9) describes how he had a vision on the road to Damascus and was temporarily struck blind. It changed his life. It changed his attitudes. He became equally zealous to spread his new faith.

In many ways, Paul's experience was typical of that of other famous individuals who have been 'converted'. For a long time Paul resisted a belief which was forcing itself upon him – in his case, by persecuting those who held it. The change of mind (*metanoia*), when it came, was sudden and decisive. It was, says the story in Acts, as though 'scales fell from Saul's eyes'. He never looked back.

The impact of St Augustine's conversion

The conversion of St Augustine was immensely important to the future of the Christian faith in the West. Augustine was a great writer. He was prolific. For 40 years as Bishop of Hippo in north Africa, he was to pour out books, sermons and letters. In these, he explored for the first time, for Latin speakers and citizens of Western Europe, a number of key questions of the Christian faith. For example, he was the first to ask what it could mean to say that every human being since Adam and Eve is a sinner. His explanation of 'original sin' was based on his observation of small children.

'My inner self was a house divided against itself.'

AUGUSTINE, *CONFESSIONS*, VIII.8

The conversion of St Augustine

Augustine of Hippo (354–430) lived at a time when Christianity had become the official religion of Roman society, but there were still many alternatives open to an enquiring young man. Augustine's mother was a Christian, but his father was a pagan – and the young Augustine resisted his mother's attempts to bring him up in her faith. He found parts of the Bible crude in their contents and style. Christianity seemed an unsophisticated choice, and unsuitable for a budding professor of rhetoric.

Augustine spent his youth trying out the other religious options of his day: philosophy, magic and, especially, the system of the 'dualist' Manichees. The Manichees seemed to him to hold out a solution to the question of how the world began. They believed that there was both a good god and an evil god, who were at war throughout eternity for control of the universe. Matter, and the material world, was the creation of the evil god and the good god was responsible only for what was spiritual. Augustine remained an adherent of this sect for nearly 10 years.

It was not until he had various disillusioning experiences, which undermined his respect for the Manichees, that Augustine grew restless. He left his native north Africa in search of career advancement, in Italy. He was impressed when he heard Bishop Ambrose of Milan preach.

Now he found himself 'pursued' by a Christian faith which eventually captured him in Milan. He had with him the New Testament book of Romans and he heard a child's voice singing in the garden next door, 'Take and read'. So he looked at the book and read the first passage his eye lighted on, and suddenly he found that the priorities of his life had shifted and he had become a Christian.

He describes in his *Confessions* how two infants behave like rivals at the breast, each jealous of the other's getting his share of the milk.

He also tells the story of an episode in his own childhood when he and a gang of other small boys stole pears from a tree, not because they were nice to eat (for they were rather small and bitter), but for the sheer devilment of the stealing.

This kind of thing was proof enough for Augustine of an inherent tendency to do wrong, gratuitous wrong, habitual wrong, in every human from the moment of birth. The vividness of his account captured the Western imagination, and his picture of human sinfulness, which he expanded in

'I have myself seen jealousy in a baby.'

AUGUSTINE,
CONFESSIONS, 1.8

a series of writings, became the accepted one, even though there were many who disagreed with him in his own day. Pelagius, for example, was a fashionable society preacher who led Roman families to believe that being good was simply a matter of trying hard. Augustine's more gloomy view was that it was beyond human power to overcome sin, and that God's help was essential. There emerged a doctrine of the need for 'divine grace', the 'free gift of God', if anyone was to overcome sin and become fit for heaven. We shall see how important this was to be in the centuries which followed.

It is important, too, that Augustine was doing this in Latin. Early Christian civilization was predominantly Greek, and the Greek language was naturally better fitted than the Latin (which is much more 'concrete') for the exploration of ideas of a theoretical and 'spiritual' sort. Augustine stretched and enlarged the capacities of Latin as a theological language. His creation of a solid 'Latin tradition', covering much of the scope of Christian belief, was crucial at a time when the knowledge of Greek was beginning to die away in the West. Since the Roman empire had extended through Greek-speaking territories, educated Romans had been expected to speak Greek, too. Now that the empire was under pressure from barbarian invaders, and was beginning to disintegrate, that expectation was becoming less realistic. Augustine himself complained that he could never really master Greek. So one of the effects of his conversion, and the life and work which followed, was to make it possible for a strong and developed Western tradition of the faith to become established.

'In an instant as I came to the end of the sentence, it was as though the light of confidence flooded into my heart and all the darkness of doubt was dispelled.'

AUGUSTINE,
CONFESSIONS, VIII.8

Conversion by mission

Once we move beyond the period of the late Roman empire, the question of what 'conversion' means begins to look different. It must be assumed that some still experienced these profound personal shifts of commitment and priority, but we do not hear from them for a few centuries.

The collapse of the old Roman political and social

Opposite page: St Augustine in the garden at Milan, at the moment of his conversion. Fresco by Chiesa degli Eremitani, Padua.

structures meant that Europe became fragmented. It was 'run' by a variety of tribes, each making its own compromise with the existing structures or sweeping them aside, as it chose. Some of the invaders were 'Arians', that is, Christian heretics who found it difficult to accept the divinity of Christ and his full equality as the Son of God with the other persons of the Trinity. That meant that the Christian faith was no longer a 'unity' in Europe for a time. Other invaders were not Christians at all, so the task at this time became one of the fresh conversion of territories which had been officially 'Christian' since the fourth century.

'Conversion by mission' is exemplified in the reconversion of the British Isles, where there is archaeological evidence that there had been Christians in Roman times. The Celtic Christians who persisted in Ireland favoured a 'charismatic' missionary method. They trusted themselves to frail boats and let the sea carry them where the Holy Spirit intended them to go. They then set about converting whoever they found when they landed. This resulted in conversion of the north of England to a Celtic Christianity.

St Columba landed in 563 on the island of Iona in the Hebrides. There, he founded a monastery, which was to be a powerhouse of Celtic influence. Missionaries went out from the monastery to Scotland and the north of England. It became a centre of learning and a place of pilgrimage.

Meanwhile, at the end of the sixth century, Pope Gregory I (Gregory the Great) is said to have seen fair Anglo-Saxons for sale as slaves in a Roman market. The story was that he cried, 'Not Angles but Angels', and was moved to send a mission to convert the people of their land to the Christian faith. His chosen missionary was Augustine of Canterbury (not a writer like his namesake). In 597, Augustine went to England and preached to the king of Kent, Ethelbert. Ethelbert was receptive, for his wife had been a Christian before she married.

Conversions of this sort may make a kingdom or state nominally Christian, but the accounts which survive of

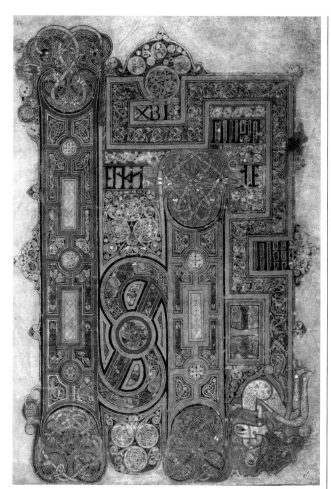

The Christians in
Celtic lands
produced books
of exceptional
beauty. This
opening of
Mark's Gospel is
from the *Book of
Kells*.

them are not as personal as those of the apostle Paul or
Augustine of Hippo. They tell us very little about the degree
to which a real understanding of, and commitment to, the
faith penetrated into the minds and hearts of the people.

This kind of missionary activity continued, moving east
across the European subcontinent during several of the
early medieval centuries, until gradually the whole of
Europe was brought into the 'fold'. Once Christianity was

The modern
abbey which
continues the
ancient monastic
tradition of Iona.

established and accepted as the 'official religion' once more, there was little by way of conscious objection. Hardly anyone would say, if asked, that he or she was an agnostic or atheist. There was, however, a good deal of argument about points of belief and practice, so there was no shortage of dissidence, as we shall see.

One example survives from the late 11th century of an author who shows that there was still some understanding of the deeper meaning of 'conversion'. Guibert of Nogent wrote an autobiography, in itself a very unusual thing to do in the

'In this year Pope Gregory sent Augustine to Britain with very many monks who preached God's word to the English nation.'

ANGLO-SAXON
CHRONICLE,
NINTH CENTURY

Middle Ages. In this, *On my Life*, he describes how when he was young his mother had found him a schoolmaster (again, an unusual privilege) and he had learned to love reading and writing poetry and reading under the bedclothes when he was supposed to be asleep. In due course, his mother followed a fashion of the nobility of that generation, and 'retired' to monastic life in maturity. This was a significant change from the many centuries in which the norm was for parents to place a small child in a monastery.

It meant that the recruits to the religious life were making a real choice, and expressing a deepened faith. Guibert realizes this, and he describes his own 'conversion', when he decided that he, too, would forsake these seductive literary pleasures and become a monk. So, for Guibert, there was a conscious choice between a lukewarm and an impassioned Christianity.

Conversion of the Jews

One more aspect of medieval 'conversion' needs a glance before we move on. There survive several 'dialogues' and other accounts of attempts to convert the Jews. Jews living in medieval Christian communities evidently fell into conversation with their neighbours, and the result was vigorous debate. Both sides were aware that they worshipped the same God and shared some of the same scriptures. The sticking-point was the Christians' insistence that Jesus was the Son of God. The Jews said that this made the Christians polytheists. There are no Christian records of Christians being converted to Judaism by these arguments, but there is a frank autobiographical account by a Jew called Hermannus of his conversion to Christianity.

The scheme of things: the cosmos

Faith in the West in the Middle Ages looked, just as it did in the Greek-speaking half of the old Roman empire, to an eternity beyond this life. Ideas of heaven were intensely real, and a comfort to those whose lot on earth was lowly or unpleasant. This 'heavenly mindedness' was an important factor in the comparative lack of interest in improving social conditions, which runs as an unbroken thread through most of the Middle Ages. Christianity taught ordinary people that acceptance and obedience to authority were virtues which would get them to heaven, where a far better life awaited them. The richer and more powerful learned that their duty was to use their wealth to help widows and orphans, and the rest of the poor and needy. The only groups of believers with any sustained interest in social reform were the dissidents, such as the Waldensians and the Lollards whom we shall meet later. Their concern was much more to challenge the 'establishment' than to replace it with a more egalitarian society.

The Bible gives one description of the kind of 'place' in which God intends his human creation to dwell. This is the Garden of Eden at the beginning of the book of Genesis.

Adam and Eve were created to live in the 'garden' with the rest of creation. This was, above all, an orderly place, in which the first human beings were free to do anything which did not involve disobedience to the will of God, and in which there were no discomforts such as mosquitoes and thistles. (Those apparently came later, after the 'fall', when Adam and Eve sinned by acting against the divine will [Genesis 3:14–24]).

Adam and Eve were driven out of this garden after their first and decisive act of sin. This set in train in the Christian tradition a theme of exile and wandering, in which Christians could envisage themselves as living their lives in a search for the garden and in an attempt to deserve to be allowed to return to it.

This was also the Jewish legacy, of course, since the Jews also accepted Genesis as scripture. But the Jews had a different concept of the implications of the sin of Adam and Eve from that which developed in Christianity. For Christians, this was so central that it explained why God had sent his Son to be born as a man and to die on the cross. The Jewish tradition preferred to look forward to the coming of a messiah who would rule a better world, in which there would be peace and plenty, no war, and in which everyone would be righteous and law-abiding.

Three kinds of heaven
Anselm of Canterbury made an unusual contribution to the medieval collection of images of heaven in the last chapters of his *Proslogion*, written late in the 11th century. This book contains his famous argument for the existence of God, and the theme of the end of a Christian's journey came in naturally at the close. Anselm reassured his readers that they would be able to go on enjoying in eternity every innocent pleasure of the present life. For example, if they enjoyed running in this life, they would be able to run faster than ever in heaven. This was a useful clarification of the role of the body in the life to come. It was the Christian belief that human

Adam and Eve are sent out of the Garden of Eden into exile. These figures express the agony of their realization of the seriousness of sin. *Expulsion of Adam and Eve from Paradise* by Tommaso Masaccio.

beings were not just spiritual beings, but souls and bodies united, and that there will be a resurrection of the body in some form, so that they could spend eternity as 'whole people'.

The other useful lesson of Anselm's description of heaven in *Proslogion* was that heaven would be fun. It answered neatly the objection that heaven sounded pleasant, but dull. Anselm was confident that heaven was not merely to be a place of rest, but a place of strong enjoyment. This was his own idea, but it also echoed the more earthly picture, by the Roman author Pindar, of a heaven in which there would be pleasant surroundings, games, music and good company – a notion also found in the Qur'an and attractive to Muslims. There was also the 'heavenly Jerusalem', more easily 'pictured' by ordinary people, and sometimes apparently confused with the Jerusalem on earth to which pilgrims could actually travel.

Both these pictures of heaven were fairly easy for people to understand and to be attracted to. But the underlying idea was sterner, more cerebral, and also more profoundly spiritual. Ideas of what 'the blessed life' would consist of were also derived, in part, from ancient philosophy. The theme of the pursuit of happiness had encouraged a good deal of discussion about what true happiness was. Augustine of Hippo wrote one of his first books on this subject, *On the Blessed Life*, soon after his conversion, when he had retired with a few friends to spend time at Cassiciacum on Lake Como in northern Italy, thinking through the ways in which his new faith required him to revise his old ideas.

Augustine's was a rather intellectual heaven, whose pleasures would consist in conversation with one's companions about spiritual things, the contemplation of truth, beauty and goodness and, above all, the joy of gazing into the mind of God and meeting him personally in an exchange of mutual understanding which would raise the creature as high as it was capable of reaching, in an eternal rapture. A few Christians in the Middle Ages claimed to have had a foretaste of that rapture in brief moments of mystical experience, when they felt as though they had been snatched out of their bodies and carried beyond this life.

In Boethius's *Consolation of Philosophy*, written in the fifth century, Boethius wrote as a person facing the final crisis of his life. He was under house arrest, and condemned to death by his political enemies. As he awaited his end, he wrote a fictional conversation with Philosophy, who is personified as though she were a goddess. This is the more striking since there is good evidence that he was a Christian (he wrote several short books on Christian themes). A good deal of the conversation is about fate, fortune and the role of providence. It was a very interesting question to philosophers and Christians alike whether there was a power in the universe in control of the ultimate outcome of events. Christians were confident that their God was omnipotent and wholly good, and would bring all things to their perfect fruition and conclusion in the end.

Thinking about these things made Boethius concentrate on his prospects of eternal life. Boethius describes eternity as 'the complete possession of a life which does not end'. This, he explains, is quite different from life in time. In eternity, we do not have yesterday and tomorrow before us at the same time as today. God is not more 'ancient' than eternity in the sense that he comes before it in time; that is impossible, since there is no time in eternity. He is somehow 'prior' to eternity in the 'simplicity' of his nature. In other words, all created things which come from God are multiple and fallible. He alone is single and unchanging.

The characteristic medieval development of this rather 'philosophical' line of thought about eternal life was to shift the emphasis towards the Christian's relationship with God himself. This is to be found in the writings of such 12th-century monks as William of St Thierry. William's God is intensely personal, but he

also has these abstract and philosophical attributes. The monk, who gives up his whole life to prayer and to a special dedication to God, is portrayed as already in heaven, for that is what he will be doing for eternity. His cell is a microcosm of heaven itself. He may have a foretaste of that heavenly experience in moments of rapture, when he seems to be snatched out of his body and carried off to heaven to be, for an instant, in the intensity of the direct presence of God.

All these ideas of heaven were linked with the concept of a 'golden age', which pagan thinkers of the classical period had also shared. For the Christian, the golden age was to be the heaven of being back in the state in which God created Adam and Eve to enjoy, and eternally enjoying the loving presence of God and the companionship of other blessed beings.

Hell

Coupled with this 'heavenly mindedness' was a general assumption that the universe was arranged hierarchically by the God who created it. With heaven went a hell. In the New Testament, the story of Lazarus the beggar tells that when he dies he is carried to heaven by the angels. He is depicted as sitting 'beside Abraham at the feast in heaven' (Luke 16:19–31), from where both gaze at the rich man who is suffering in hell. The rich man is told that he has had his time of prosperity. Now it is Lazarus' turn. And, moreover, there is no passing between heaven and hell. The rich man is in hell, without hope, for eternity.

This story encapsulates the pervasive medieval attitude that the heavenly future was more important than improving social conditions (even if the rich man should have helped Lazarus). But it also creates a strong image of heaven and hell as places, one above the other, in a cosmic hierarchy. Both aspects are present in Augustine of Hippo's book, *The City of God*, towards the end of which he reflects on the pleasure that those in heaven will take in the contemplation of the sufferings of those in hell, for

Opposite page: Christ as king in the heavenly Jerusalem. He is surrounded by the symbols of the four evangelists and citizens of heaven in their appointed places. Medieval parchment from Hradcany Castle, Prague.

they will reflect on the extraordinary mercy of God in rescuing them from the fate which they also deserved as sinners.

Angels

In the Middle Ages, it was clearly understood that the angels were a separate creation of purely spiritual rational beings. Their creation is not mentioned anywhere in the Bible, and they were usually 'inserted' in the story in Genesis at the point at which the light was separated from darkness. Angels and archangels appear in several places in the Bible, and in chapter 6 of the book of Isaiah there is a description of the seraphim. These have six wings, two of which they use to cover their faces, two of which they use to cover their bodies and two of which they use to fly.

There was a hierarchy of nine 'orders' of angels, too, derived from the writings of the fifth-century Dionysius the Areopagite. The Greek word *angelos* means 'messenger'. Ordinary angels were at the bottom of the hierarchy – mere messengers to mortals. Archangels were above them, charged with delivering more important messages. The Archangel Gabriel, for example, brought the news to the Virgin Mary that she was to be the mother of the Son of God, and Michael the Archangel is quoted in verse 9 of the book of Jude. At the top of the hierarchy were the seraphim, who spent eternity before the throne of God in adoring contemplation, and just below them were the cherubim. (Medieval cherubim were not simply the chubby babies of Renaissance art, but creatures of high spiritual dignity.) Between these highest and lowest ranks came five other ranks of angels: powers, dominions, thrones, virtues and principalities.

In some 12th-century writings there is an attempt to equate these nine orders of angels with a hierarchy of humans. The idea was that, in eternity, human monks and nuns, who had given their lives to contemplation, could expect to be 'placed' in heaven alongside the contemplative

Dante's heaven and hell

The most extensive medieval geography and sociology of heaven and hell is to be found in the 13th-century poet Dante's *Divine Comedy*. This narrative poem describes Dante's own journey through the cosmos, in a vision. It gives a clear hierarchical and moral 'structure' to the universe.

Dante's guide through hell is the Roman poet Virgil. The companions move onwards, travelling through different levels of hell until they reach a 'place' – an 'invention' of the 12th century – called 'purgatory'. 'Place' should not have been used literally, since heaven and hell were believed in the Middle Ages to be 'in eternity' and, therefore, outside the world of space and time. But, in the case of purgatory, it was appropriate because the purpose of purgatory was to provide a waiting-room for heaven, in which time still existed. Most

people died with sins on their souls. Even if they had confessed their sins and been forgiven by a priest, they had still not completed the penances imposed by the Church.

These penances were a token of repentance, and it was held very firmly in the Middle Ages that God had entrusted the Church with the authority to impose penances, and that God expected them to be discharged. A period in purgatory was seen as a method of discharging penances after death, so that the dead person became 'holy' and fit for heaven.

The last and highest place Dante comes to is heaven itself. Here, Virgil cannot accompany him as his guide, because he is not a Christian. Dante meets a new guide, Beatrice. Her name means 'blessed' and she is, therefore, a very suitable person to lead him into the realms where she herself dwells. But even Beatrice cannot take Dante to the highest levels of heaven. The levels of heaven empty out into metaphysics, a realm which is truly 'super'-natural.

Dante is shown holding a copy of his *Divine Comedy*, while behind him in the landscape people can be seen trying to climb up to heaven. To his left is a vision of hell. By Domenico Michelino (15th century).

angels. Kings could expect to find themselves with the thrones or principalities, and so on.

The fall of the angels

The relationship of people and angels as God's rational creatures was an idea which derived from the need to answer the puzzle of what happened to God's plan when some of the angels 'fell'. Their fall was not like the fall of Adam and Eve and, like the creation of the angels, it is not described in the Bible. It was a rationalization of a number of elements which required explanation. God could not be the author of evil, yet evil was obviously a very powerful force. We shall come later to the cluster of heresies which tried to struggle with this problem. But it was not difficult to point to the agent of evil in the world if it was suggested that one of the highest of the angels had turned against God and sought power for himself. The 'turning', said Anselm of Canterbury, consisted in wanting something which it was good to want (to be like God), but wanting it to a degree which was not appropriate for a mere creature. So there developed an understanding that Lucifer, or Satan, was a fallen angel, with a mission to seduce other spiritual beings and to deprive God of his people. One of the features of evil was that it twisted people and made them behave in irrational and destructive ways.

The fall of Satan and his followers could not be allowed to frustrate God's plan for the universe, for God is omnipotent. God intended there to be a heaven with a certain number of blessed spirits in it, so ran the medieval expectation. This gave a reason for the creation of human beings, to fill the gaps, and it also explained why Satan was so keen to frustrate this rescue attempt by seducing Adam and Eve. There resulted from this line of thought a picture of heaven in which the blessed were like living stones (1 Peter 2:5), forming the very fabric of the 'temple' of heaven, alongside the good angels.

The medieval hierarchy of the rest of creation ran downwards from the spiritual to the inanimate. Angels are pure spirit and capable of reasoning. Human beings also have rational minds, but their souls inhabit bodies. Animals are not rational, but they live and move. The vegetable creation lives, but it does not move. Stones and rocks simply exist. These facts about the world seemed so solid to medieval people that the reality and divine purpose of hierarchical arrangements in general seem to have been little questioned.

C H A P T E R   2

What Did Medieval Christians Believe?

W hen Christ died, Christianity faced the test which always arises when a great religious leader is no longer present in person. It had to become a system of belief and acquire some organizational structure, or it could not survive.

Medieval Christians got the 'content' of their faith from two main sources: the Bible, and that process of synthesis of a more or less systematic set of beliefs which took place in the Church in the early Christian centuries. This was a complex process. It involved debates, out of which some people emerged labelled as dissidents and heretics. It involved holding councils to take formal decisions about what was considered 'orthodox' and what was not, and about the influence of the underlying theology of the sequence of events in acts of worship (liturgy). It involved a great deal of subtle borrowing and adjustment, taking in certain elements from contemporary philosophy and from Judaism.

The Christian synthesis
Christianity was solidly resistant to 'syncretism' in the early Christian centuries. This meant that it would not compromise with the numerous polytheistic and 'philosophical' religions around it. It suffered persecution as a consequence. Resisting the intellectual trends of the day, however, was another matter, for these were not rival religions, but part of the cultural 'furniture' of the lives of educated people. For many generations, intellectuals 'doing philosophy' had taken 'philosophy' to include

much of the area of discourse in which Christians were interested.

First, they saw philosophy as 'moral' philosophy. They tried to use their study of philosophical ideas as a basis for living a good life. Out of this emphasis, which was particularly influenced by the Stoics, came a tendency to value the preservation of tranquillity and moderation (or the avoidance of excess), and self-denial. These were especially Greek contributions. A conscientious attention to public service was expected by the Romans, and Cicero wrote in that vein.

Secondly, many topics with which the early Christians struggled were familiar ground in the philosophical debates of ancient Greece and Rome. This was the group of issues gathered together by Boethius in his 'theological treatises' in the sixth century, and they were most strongly influenced by Plato and his successors. They comprised, first, ideas about the nature and attributes of God: his transcendence, so high that he was perhaps to be thought of as beyond even 'being'; his beauty, truth, justice, mercy, so great that these were not really mere 'attributes' at all – they were of God's very substance.

Next came ideas about the triune nature of God – the Christian Trinity of Father, Son and Holy Spirit. There had been a good deal of discussion among 'Platonists' in the ancient world about the way in which a supreme being so high that he rose even above being itself could have any communication with the world we live in. It was suggested that there was a *logos*, or rational principle, somehow 'speaking' God's 'ideas'; and a 'soul of the world', which put them into action in the physical environment of the created world. The essential characteristic of this trio was that it was hierarchical. It formed a ladder leading down from God to the world. The *anima mundi*, or world-soul, was thought by some to be, itself, part of the world.

One of the most important tasks of early Christianity was to insist that the Father, Son and Holy Spirit, which bore some obvious resemblance to this triad of the philosophers, formed in fact a 'Trinity' of persons who were equal, co-eternal and divine. There was never a 'time' when the Father was not the Father of the Son. Although, in human relationships, sons are younger than fathers and junior to them, that is not the way it is with God. The Son is of the same substance with the Father, and in no way his inferior. When the Son was born as the man Jesus, he was already, eternally, the Son of the Father.

This is not at all easy to grasp, and throughout the early centuries and the Middle Ages attempts were made to find 'images' to help. St Patrick's famous comparison with the shamrock is one. He is said to have held up the three little leaves joined in one leaf and said that the Trinity was like that. A more abstract idea is to be found in Augustine's words, and adapted by Anselm. This compares God to a stream of water, where the water is all one 'substance', but there is a 'source' or 'spring' where the water begins, a stream and a pool into which the stream empties itself. These are compared to the Father, Son and Holy Spirit.

Third in the group of themes common to Christianity and ancient philosophy was 'creation'. Here the philosophers had contributed the idea of emanation, or overflow, in which God was able to make things by an overflow of his goodness.

This sort of thing had the attraction of being very interesting, and it had obvious relevance to the concerns of Christians. It is possible to see Christians in every century wrestling with their consciences about how much they should 'use' such ideas and read the books which contained them. Jerome, who made the Vulgate translation of the Bible, and who lived at the end of the fourth and the beginning of the fifth centuries, became famous for his admission in one of his letters that he had had a dream in which he was accused of being 'not a Christian but a Ciceronian' (*non Christianus sed Ciceronianus*). Boethius himself wrote a good deal more about philosophy than he did about Christian theology. When he found himself in a condemned cell as a political prisoner under house arrest

The Holy Trinity
with the Father
seated, Christ on
the cross and the
Holy Spirit
descending in the
form of a dove.
Missal by Zanobi
Strozzi.

in the stormy days of the end of the Roman empire, it
was to philosophy that he turned in his reflections on the
purpose of life and the ways of fate, in his *Consolation of
Philosophy*. Medieval authors used the classics and the
ancient philosophers where they could get copies of the
books, but they generally tried to treat them as a less
authoritative form of 'authority' than the Christian
'Fathers', and certainly than the Bible itself.

But there were still periods of 'crisis' about the
use that a Christian could properly make of ancient
philosophical ideas. For example, in the early universities
of the third century, there were fierce disputes about the
influence of the scientific works of Aristotle. Long lists of
Aristotle's opinions were repeatedly 'banned' (which, of

course, had the effect of making them more interesting
still to students and scholars).

Jesus: God and man

There was, in addition, a 'body of belief' in the faith of
Christians which was not easily identified as part of that
set of religious themes already familiar to the philosophers
of the ancient world. This concerned the historical events
of the birth of Jesus, his life, death and resurrection, and
the meaning of these events. The central difficulty in the
centuries before our medieval period was to accept that
someone who was fully human could also really be God.
And yet, unless Jesus was both God and man, the Christian
religion made no sense.

To begin with, the problem was that this seemed
to demean God. Ancient philosophy had placed a strong
emphasis on the idea that the supreme being was so high
that he was almost above being itself. To bring him down
to the level of contact with the physical world he had
made was a distasteful idea. Yet the Christians said that
he actually became man in Jesus, being born of a human
female, like any other member of the human race. Some
suggested that perhaps God, in the person of Christ, merely
wore his humanity like a cloak or garment, so that he was
only 'dressed up' as a man. Augustine's friend Alypius had
that idea. The definition of Christian orthodoxy in the first
centuries following Christ's death involved the systematic
and determined rebuttal of ideas such as these.

An alternative view was to recognize that Jesus was an
exceptional human being and no more. Augustine of Hippo
says that, for a time, he himself thought of Christ in this way.

The 'grasping' of the meaning of the faith that Jesus
was the Son of God was therefore something that each
individual had to achieve for himself. It was not just a
matter of the Church making a ruling.

Thinkers of the medieval centuries continued to
struggle with this understanding. Anselm of Canterbury
wrote the *Cur Deus Homo* (*Why did God Become Man?*) to

*'Alypius thought
that Christians
believed that
God was clothed
in the flesh...
He did not
think that their
teaching was
that Christ had
a human
mind... Later
on he realized
that this was the
error of the
Apollinarian
heretics.'*

AUGUSTINE,
CONFESSIONS, VII.19

try to show his generation why, logically, God must truly have become man. He assumes that the universe is like the kind of feudal kingdom with which he is familiar, where the king can be dishonoured by disobedience. He explains that when Adam and Eve disobeyed God they created a situation where honour required that something was done to put that right. For Anselm, this is a matter of the deepest 'order' of the universe. 'Right order' (*rectus ordo*) is a favourite theme of his.

The creeds

'Faith in Christ' began in the lifetime of Jesus, when he attracted the followers who were known first as 'disciples' (pupils), and then as 'apostles' (missionaries), because he sent them out on a mission to teach others. This was faith in a person.

A 'creed' is something different. It is a statement of faith. The word comes from the Latin *credo*, 'I believe', which was the first word of the creed, and which also gave it its name. But it was important that Christians said the creed together in worship, as they still do. It is really '*we* believe' (*credimus*). There was a strong emphasis in the early Church on the 'community of faith'. There was a single 'faith' which everyone held, and which distinguished true Christians from those of other religions and from those Christians who, from time to time, adopted 'erroneous opinions'. The faith of the community of Christians was set out in the creeds in a brief, but official form.

This was important in the late Roman world. The pattern of Roman conquest had always involved a simple 'amalgamation' of whatever religions were found in the conquered territories with the pantheon of Rome's pagan gods. So, in Greece, Zeus, the king of the gods, was identified with Jupiter. Hera was identified with Juno, the queen of the gods, and so on. Such syncretism was not, however, acceptable to Christians or Jews. While the Jews could 'know who they were' relatively easily, through family

'I thought of Christ, my Lord, as no more than a man of extraordinary wisdom, whom none could equal. In particular, I saw his miraculous birth of a virgin mother... as an act of the divine providence which looks after us, so that by it he merited his special authority as our Teacher. But I had not even an inkling of the meaning of the mystery of the Word made flesh.'

AUGUSTINE,
CONFESSIONS, VII.19

heritage, the new Christians had to 'define' themselves and discover their identity as a group of believers. They acclaimed their shared faith in Jesus and, in particular, their certainty that he had been resurrected from the dead.

This did not mean that the idea of faith as an individual's personal position, the commitment in trust of each separate person to Jesus, became secondary. There

A Greek Orthodox mosaic of the resurrection, at the end of the world, when Christ brings the dead back to life and the tombs and graves burst open.

remained a moment of personal decision when a new Christian was baptized and, before that, a long process of study of the faith, which was known as the catechumenate. In the early Church, the catechumens would sit in a separate group in church and leave before the eucharist, so the Christian community was very conscious of them as not yet quite 'members'. But at the end of the fourth century, there was a change of practice, and it became usual in the West to baptize infants as soon as possible after they were born. The reason for this was a strengthening of the doctrine that baptism took away both the guilt and the penalty of original sin. Augustine taught that an infant who died unbaptized would be damned for eternity. So it became extremely urgent to make sure. As a result, this visible 'separateness' of those who did not yet 'belong' disappeared. There was, as a result, perhaps even a strengthening of the sense of community, for the members of a Christian family were also members of the Church from the beginning of their lives.

The balance between 'I believe' and 'we believe' was not a matter of controversy in the Middle Ages. When every child of a Christian family, which meant most of the population, was baptized in early infancy, it was taken for granted that individuals could join in the 'we believe', as well as say their own 'I believe'. That did not mean, of course, that they necessarily all believed it with the same liveliness and commitment. Instruction was patchy and worship was in Latin throughout the Middle Ages, long after Latin was the normal everyday language of ordinary people, so it is hard to be sure how much of their faith people really understood. We shall look at this question of the theological sophistication of the laity later on.

Alongside the idea of faith as a state or condition of the soul, a loving trust in God and a commitment to God, stands the question what exactly it *was* that Christians believed. What was the *content* of this belief? This was set out in the creeds themselves. The two most important versions of the creed in use in the Middle Ages (and still in use today) have quite different origins.

The Apostles' Creed

The 'Apostles' Creed' had the great attraction for medieval users of being thought to be the work of the apostles themselves. In its present form, it is first found in the eighth century, but it is certainly older, with versions in local use from at least the fourth century. It may go back to the first period of the Roman Church. It was known as the *symposium* because of a story, which was in circulation from about the end of the fourth century, that the apostles sat together around a table to make it up, each contributing a clause.

No council of the Church formally approved the Apostles' Creed. It gained its currency from its use and acceptance, and gained its authority from the belief that it was the work of Jesus' own apostles. It was used in the Middle Ages in the baptism service, and was thus important as a statement of the beliefs of the candidate for baptism.

The Nicene Creed

The Nicene Creed was approved by the Council of Nicea in 325, in a period of active controversy. It was amended by the Council of Constantinople in 381. Its main contents are really much older, and probably derive from the baptismal creed of ancient Christian Jerusalem, or something similar. In the late fifth century, the custom seems to have begun of reciting the Nicene Creed after the gospel had been read in the eucharist, or holy communion. Like the Apostles' Creed, it was regularly used in worship and became extremely familiar.

An ecumenical experiment?

A new clause, the *filioque* clause, was added to the Nicene Creed in the West in the eighth century. The line which reads, 'Who proceeds from the Father and the Son' originally read, 'Who proceeds from the Father'. The addition caused great offence in the Eastern half of medieval Christendom, because the Greeks would not allow any change to the original formulation. Their objection seems to have been more to the innovation than to the substance of the addition itself, though both became matters of fierce controversy for many centuries after 1054, when the two halves of Christendom became divided. Anselm of Canterbury was asked by the pope at the Council of Bari in 1098 to explain to the Greeks who were there why the Western view was 'right'. Anselm, Bishop of Havelberg, went to Constantinople in the mid-12th century and held 'ecumenical conversations' with Greek Christian leaders there. His *Dialogues*, reporting the results, still survive. They show how far apart the 'mindset' of East and West had now grown, as Anselm of Havelberg wrote his account in Latin for the Western readers who would understand 'Western' assumptions best.

The most significant official attempt to resolve the difference of opinion was the Council of Florence, which was held in a series of Italian cities – Ferrara, Florence and Rome – between 1438 and 1445. The Patriarch of

A mosaic of
Christ in majesty
('Pantocrator' or
'Ruler of all'),
from Cefalu
Cathedral.

Constantinople attended. Bessarion, Archbishop of Nicea, and Mark of Ephesus were the leading theologians from the East. Bessarion achieved something in tune with 20th-century ecumenical methodology in his *Dogmatic Discourse*. He tried to show that the East and the West had always really taught the same thing. There was even a provisional agreement on the part of the Greeks at the Council to accept the pope as universal Primate.

The agreement foundered, however, when the Eastern bishops took it home and put it to their synods. The Greek Church 'on the ground' did not recognize the proposals as their own. This is a common phenomenon in ecumenical dialogue. Those involved in trying to reach an agreement gain one another's confidence and recognize all sorts of subtleties as a result of talking hard and cooperatively; those who have not been involved find it difficult to enter into what has happened and to 'own' the result.

There was another important 'structural' reason why the agreement of the Council of Florence did not mend the Schism between the Greek East and the Latin West. In the West, the Bishop of Rome, as pope, was head of the whole structure. However, in the East, each of the ancient patriarchs (of Antioch, Alexandria, Constantinople and Jerusalem) led an 'autocephalous' section of the Church – a section with its own head. Although these sectors agreed in one faith, they were self-determining in many ways. So when they said that they would not accept the outcome of the Council of Florence, this great medieval ecumenical experiment failed. Even today, this division is still not mended.

A picture of the crucifixion of Christ from a book belonging to King Louis of France in the 13th century.

The development of theology

The problem caused by the *filioque* clause was one of the earliest medieval examples of the way in which a change of wording, or a sudden realization of what familiar words might mean, could throw up a challenge to belief. This could be a quite different matter from the heresy and dissidence we shall be looking at in a later chapter.

Debates about the faith developed in the Middle Ages as new areas of interest were opened up and new aspects of doctrine were fully defined for the first time. This made the Middle Ages an important period, particularly in the development of a doctrine of the sacraments and in the theology of the Church.

The beginning of academic theology is also to be found in the Middle Ages, with the rise of the universities. In the late 11th century, there was a spurt of enthusiasm for advanced study. Young men began to travel Europe in search of the wandering teachers who would lecture to them not only on grammar (the theory of language), but also on logic (formal reasoning) and rhetoric (methods of putting arguments persuasively). These formed the subjects of the classical *trivium* ('three ways') and, together with what Boethius first called the *quadrivium*, the (less fully

The Apostles' Creed

I believe in God the Father Almighty, Maker of heaven and earth:
And in Jesus Christ his only Son our Lord,
Who was conceived by the Holy Ghost,
Born of the Virgin Mary,
Suffered under Pontius Pilate,
Was crucified, dead, and buried:
He descended into hell;
The third day he rose again from the dead;
He ascended into heaven,
And sitteth on the right hand of God the Father Almighty;
From thence he shall come to judge the quick and the dead.
I believe in the Holy Ghost;
the holy Catholic church;
the Communion of Saints;
the forgiveness of sins;
the resurrection of the body;
and the life everlasting.

studied) mathematical subjects of arithmetic, geometry, music and astronomy, they made up the 'seven liberal arts'. They had been studied in a relatively elementary way since the fall of the Roman empire, but never before had more advanced study been applied systematically to the study of Christian beliefs, as now began to happen.

The Nicene Creed

I believe in one God the Father Almighty,
Maker of heaven and earth,
And of all things visible and invisible;
And in one Lord Jesus Christ, the only-begotten Son of God,
Begotten of his Father before all worlds,
God of God, light of light,
Very God of very God,
Begotten not made,
Being of one substance with the Father,
By whom all things were made;
Who for us men and for our salvation came down from heaven,
And was incarnate by the Holy Ghost of the Virgin Mary,
And was made man,
And was crucified also for us under Pontius Pilate,
He suffered and was buried, and the third day he rose again according to the
      Scriptures,
And ascended into heaven,
And sitteth on the right hand of the Father.
And he shall come again with glory to judge both the quick and the dead:
Whose Kingdom shall have no end.
And I believe in the Holy Ghost
The Lord and giver of life,
Who proceedeth from the Father and the Son,
Who with the Father and the Son together is worshipped and glorified,
Who spake by the prophets.
And I believe in one catholic and apostolic church.
I acknowledge one baptism for the remission of sins.
And I look for the resurrection of the dead, and the life of the world to come.
Amen.

As an example, in logic, one of the Aristotelian textbooks was *The Categories*. In it, Aristotle lists 10 'categories' under which anything can be analyzed or defined, so that when it is referred to in argument there is no confusion about exactly what it is. He says that everything has a substance, which can have various attributes (quantity, quality, time, place and so on). One of these is 'relation'. The essence of this system is that everything about a given thing, except for its substance, can change. For instance, I remain human even if I get fatter or thinner (quantity), my hair turns grey (quality), it is today rather than tomorrow that you are considering me (time) and whether I am at home or in the street (place).

The sole exception to this, said the Christian student, is God himself. In God, all these 'accidental' things are not accidental at all. They do not change. God's goodness and mercy (qualities) are of his very substance. God is infinite, and that is not a quantity – it is his very substance. He is eternal, and that is not a 'time' – it is his very substance. But, as Augustine of Hippo and Boethius both realized, there is one 'category' which poses special problems with reference to God, and that is 'relation'. If I am a father or a son, I am in 'relation' to my son or to my father. In that relationship, the son is not the father, and the father is not the son. In the Godhead, the Son is as old as the Father and their relationship never had a 'beginning'. This conundrum was studied afresh in the 11th and 12th centuries.

There was added to this another 'theological puzzle' arising out of *The Categories*. This concerned what happened when a priest consecrated the bread and wine in the service of the eucharist, or holy communion, in memory of what Jesus did at the Last Supper with his disciples. Did the bread and wine turn literally into the body and blood of Christ when the priest said the words, 'This is my body' and 'This is my blood'? Medieval Christians came to a clear belief that they did, once the doctrine of 'transubstantiation' had been worked out.

Berengar of Tours, a controversial figure of the late 11th century, had claimed that the change was merely 'spiritual'. That prompted the Church's apologists to react angrily and to insist on the most extreme literalism. This amounted to turning Aristotle's *Categories* on its head. Normally, a loaf grows mouldy; its 'quality' changes, but it is still bread. In the eucharist, the faith said, the outward appearance of the bread (its quality) remains the same, but its very substance changes from that of bread to that of the actual body of Christ. Whether this doctrine is correct has remained a subject of debate, but its importance here is that it illustrates the way in which academic study of secular subjects could affect thinking about the Christian faith.

The heated arguments generated by these debates created a certain competitiveness among the Masters, who were lecturing to a suddenly burgeoning number of students. The Masters favoured places which had an existing 'school' because these made natural centres for students to congregate. Here, one Master could woo another's students with comparative ease.

The cathedrals had all been required to have schools for their canons since Charlemagne's time (c. 742–814). Paris, in particular, was an attraction, because it had not only the cathedral school, but also the school attached to the House of Victorine Canons at St Victor. To Paris came teachers anxious to make their names, such as the ambitious Peter Abelard. As an arrogant young man who had proved himself as a logician, he was now intent on showing that he could apply these skills to theology. He had begun by attending the lectures of Anselm of Laon at the cathedral school at Laon. Abelard says in his autobiographical letter about these events that he expected a great tree of learning, but that when he came close he saw that old Anselm had nothing but bare branches to show. Abelard threw down a challenge. He said he would lecture the next day on Ezekiel, notoriously one of the most difficult of the Old Testament books to interpret.

That gave him a taste for theology, and he went on to write a series of comprehensive works on the subject.

In such ways, above all under the pressure of interest in the ways in which the study of the liberal arts could throw light on theology, the demand for higher education grew throughout the 12th century. By the beginning of the 13th century, there were recognizable 'universities' at Paris, at Oxford and Cambridge (neither of which began in proximity to a cathedral school), and elsewhere in Europe. Bologna, for example, developed a specialist interest in the teaching of law as a higher degree subject.

A medieval congregation of the 14th century. French book illumination from *Histoire du Roi d'Angleterre Richard II*.

Robert Grosseteste, who died in 1253, spent a long life in and out of these schools, particularly Oxford. In the end, he became Bishop of Lincoln. His attempt to build serious science on the story of the creation in the book of Genesis is an example of the creative theological uses to which the new learning was being put. (The story of the creation of light, for example, prompted a study of optics.)

However, the application of the enthusiasms of higher education to matters of faith was not without its problems.

A late-medieval
university scene,
in which the
scholars, in cap
and gown, seem
to be taking part
in a 'disputation'.
A copy after an
engraving
(c. 1400).

A good deal more of Aristotle's work had now become
available in Latin, particularly the scientific and
philosophical writings, as a result of the labours of
translators. With them came commentaries by the Arabic
scholars who had possessed the Aristotelian materials in

their own schools for some centuries. This led to a 13th-century university crisis about the dangers of Aristotle.

So, 'defining the faith' did not turn out to be something that could be done once and for all. The more Christians thought about it, the more they argued and, because of the almost universal recognition of its importance, they argued fiercely. These were not just academic debates. They were debates about life and death – indeed, about eternal life.

CHAPTER 3

Bible Study

C hrist died on a cross, in a crucifixion, with all the grimness of the method of execution which was favoured by the regime of the time. But three days later, his followers claimed, he rose again. This located Jesus in history. That resurrection story became the foundation-stone of a Christian faith which would continue to look to a faith in a living person. Moreover, Jesus had promised that after his ascension he would send the Holy Spirit to be a comforter to his followers, so there was a further personal presence for Christian believers to turn to (John 14:16, 26). The Jesus of the fourth Gospel, the Gospel of John, is thus the 'sender' of the Spirit, who abides in the Church.

'They crucified Jesus there, and the two criminals, one on his right and the other on his left. Jesus said, "Forgive them, Father! They don't know what they are doing."'

LUKE 23:33–34

The Word of God

The early Christian community early adopted the idea that the Son of God was the *logos*, or Word of God, through whom God created the world. John's Gospel begins with the words: 'In the beginning the Word already existed. The Word was with God, and the Word was God. From the very beginning the Word was with God. Through him God made all things; not one thing in all creation was made without him. The Word was the source of life, and this life brought light to humanity.'

There was also a strong sense of the Word as literally a 'word' – indeed, the 'words' of the Bible. The Holy Spirit had a role here, too, because it was believed that it was the Holy Spirit who entered the world to give the actual words of scripture to its human writers.

The other Gospel writers concentrated on the life history of Jesus, and the teaching he gave was presented largely in that context. Although the author of John's Gospel may have known and used the other Gospels, and perhaps some of those which told the story of Jesus' life but did not find their way into the canon of the Bible, John's emphasis was different. He concentrated on Jesus as sent from God, doing miracles and making signs. The main focus is on Jesus the teacher, or rabbi (John 1:38), and on the teaching which Jesus gave in periods of withdrawal with his disciples, not on that which was given in his public ministry. There is a link with the theme of the *logos* here, too, because it shows the reader a Christ who is not only the source of the contents of the Bible as 'given' to its human 'authors' by the Holy Spirit but, somehow, also the very Word of God himself. So, one of the ways in which the early Christian community believed

Luke the evangelist with his traditional symbol, the ox.

that it still had the living presence of Christ was through the writings which eventually formed the 'canon' of the scriptures, the books of the Bible in an agreed sequence.

The identification of Christ with the Word, and the belief that the whole text had come from God himself, lent the Bible a sacredness which no other writings could match. 'The sacred page' was studied minutely in the Middle Ages, every word weighed for significance. Bernard of Clairvaux is a particularly striking example of a writer who was almost incapable of writing a sentence without a scriptural echo in it. He was also conscientious about textual exactitude. In a 'retractation' to his treatise warning his monks how easy it was to go downhill on 'the steps of humility and pride', he says, 'I put down something by accident which I later realised was not as it is written in the gospel. The text simply says, "Nor does the Son know", but I, by mistake, forgot the actual words, though not the sense, and said, "Nor does the Son of Man know."' He explains that he built a passage of interpretation on this mistaken reading.

At the same time, the sense of presence of the Holy Spirit informed the reading of scripture. Ailred of Rievaulx, another 12th-century Cistercian monk, and Bernard's contemporary, wrote in *The Mirror of the Soul* (II.8): 'The Holy Spirit, the very will and love of God, God himself, comes and pours himself out in our hearts... completely transforming our affection into something... which is not just a clinging to him... but becoming one spirit with him, as the Apostle clearly says in the words, "The man who unites himself to the Lord becomes one spirit with him."'

The language problem

The books of the Bible took their settled form in Greek and Hebrew, two languages which few Christians in the West could speak during the Middle Ages. The Roman empire had had two main 'centres': Rome itself, and Constantinople, the city of the emperor Constantine,

which is now known as Istanbul. The language of the
Western half of the Roman empire was Latin; the
language of the Eastern part was Greek. As late as the
fourth century, educated Romans were expected to study
Greek, but that expectation gradually diminished.

As the Roman empire decayed, and barbarian invaders
destroyed its political structure, the old exchanges died
away, and by the sixth century, few Latin speakers really
had a command of the other language. It is uncertain
whether Pope Gregory the Great (590–604) had any

The Bible takes shape

The Old Testament books which were accepted as part of the Bible were not
new. They formed the Jewish scriptures. A New Testament was written during
the first centuries following Christ's death. It consists of: four Gospels (though
more were written), telling the story of the life of Jesus; a 'historical' book,
telling the story of the earliest Christians and the way in which they gathered
themselves together into churches (the Acts of the Apostles); a set of letters,
mainly to these early churches and between the leading figures of this
movement; and the Apocalypse, or book of Revelation, a prophecy about
the end of the world.

The formation of the 'canon', that is, the list of 'approved' books which the
Church accepted as scriptural, is a story in which it is apparent that the Bible and
the Church cannot easily be separated as authorities. Judaism already had the idea
of a set of texts which could be relied upon as a 'sacred literature'. The list was the
subject of debate, for the books now known as the Apocrypha, or deuterocanonical
books, never quite established their position incontrovertibly. But by the first
century the list for the Old Testament was more or less fixed. Christians took this
over and began to add books of their own. By the mid-second century, the four
Gospels and 13 letters by Paul were generally accepted as part of the body of
Christian sacred writings. However, even as late as the mid-fourth century, there
was still uncertainty about other books which are now firmly part of the New
Testament, such as Hebrews, Jude and the Apocalypse, or book of Revelation. Some
other books (the Epistle of Barnabas and the Shepherd of Hermas) were accepted
locally, but not by the Church as a whole. The texts which were admitted into the
collection as 'sacred scriptures' were confidently believed to be inspired writings,
divinely dictated word by word.

Jerome's Latin translation of the Bible

The most important version of the Bible for the West in the Middle Ages was the translation of the Bible into Latin which came to be called the Vulgate (the 'standard version'). It was translated by Jerome (c. 342–420), at the instigation of Pope Damasus. Jerome was a complex character, short-tempered and difficult to live with, but much respected as a spiritual adviser by the high-born ladies of late fourth-century Rome. Many of his letters of advice to them survive. He encouraged them to live like nuns in their homes, the widows refraining from marrying again and the daughters choosing not to marry, but to live as dedicated virgins.

St Jerome, the translator of the Bible, with his books in the desert, trying to resist temptation. *St Jerome Translating the Bible* (c. 15th century).

Jerome's new translation was needed not only because there were already signs of a language gap, but because those who wanted to read the Bible in Latin were in danger of being confused by the existence of a number of different Latin versions, some more reliable than others. Jerome tried to equip himself to consult the Hebrew original. His version was not perfect, and he himself said very clearly that he did not consider himself inspired. Nevertheless, the Vulgate was treated throughout the West for more than 1,000 years with the reverence due to the very words of God, and fine points of his Latin wording were treated as though God had intended them exactly as they were. For example, at the beginning of the book of Job (1:1) Jerome chose the translation *vir unus*, 'one man'. Commentators puzzled over this. The sentence seems to mean that there was a man living in the land of Hus whose name was Job. Why say 'one man'? The 'one' must be significant. Interpreters therefore tried hard to find a reason for the 'one'.

knowledge of Greek, even though he had spent time in Constantinople. This meant that even a highly educated Western European Christian, presented with a copy of the New Testament in Greek, had to ask for a translation. This language gap persisted until late in the Middle Ages.

For the Old Testament, too, there was the question of the Septuagint, itself a Greek version, which was, according to the story, made by 72 translators. In fact it is a work carried out over a considerable period and probably completed by the mid-second century. The text had substantial authority alongside the Hebrew original.

The lack of knowledge of Hebrew is more puzzling, in a way, because there were always communities of Jews living among the Christians in the towns and cities of Western Europe. In the Middle Ages, a few scholars went to the trouble of asking local Jews about the meaning of Hebrew words, but it was, again, not until late in the Middle Ages that it seems to have occurred to anyone to create formal courses of study so that students could learn Hebrew well enough to read the Old Testament in the original language for themselves.

What kind of book is the Bible?
Jerome's translation of the Bible, the Vulgate, did not resolve the problem of 'understanding' the Bible, which was faced by educated readers and simpler Christians alike in medieval times. The Bible is not a straightforward 'handbook to the faith'.

First, it is not one book, but a collection of separate books. That was very obvious to its readers; a complete *Biblia* in one volume was unusual. When Augustine was converted in Milan, he had just the book of Romans with him at the time.

Secondly, the Bible is a collection of many different *kinds* of books. There is history (the Acts of the Apostles), law (Leviticus), poetry (the Song of Songs) and prophecy (Elijah), as well as the Gospel stories, which describe the life and work of Jesus and his death on the cross.

'When I was a young man, though I was protected by the rampart of the lonely desert, I could not endure against the promptings of sin and the ardent heat of my nature. I tried to crush them by frequent fasting, but my mind was always in a turmoil of distracting thoughts. To subdue it I put myself in the hands of one of the brethren who had been a Hebrew before his conversion, and asked him to teach me his language.'

JEROME, LETTER 125

Opposite page:
A 13th-century
illustrated French
Bible showing
parts of the story
of Solomon.
From *Codex
Vindobonensis.*

But most importantly for the ordinary Christian reader, the Bible is not all written in a single tone of voice or style, or at the same level. It is not a systematic 'textbook'. The medieval reader explained God's purpose in 'writing' the Bible in this way (as its divine author) in terms of the human state of sinfulness. Augustine was clear that one of the effects of original sin is to make the sinner lose the clear-headedness that God intended him to have as a rational creature. The illumination of divine reasonableness goes out of his life. He becomes confused and sees things in a twisted way. So the Bible is written to meet the sinner halfway in his darkness and confusion of mind.

The many meanings of scripture

The Bible is full of apparent contradictions. For instance, not all the Gospel stories match. This presented a problem in medieval times, if it was believed that every word had been dictated by God and was, in fact, the word of God itself. God is truth and he is omnipotent, so there cannot be any mistakes. The possibility of errors was admitted in the course of the Middle Ages, but there was still no thought of criticizing the divine author. It was recognized that human scribes could make copying mistakes, and in the 13th century, there was a systematic attempt to tidy up such errors and restore the copies of the Bible then in circulation to a more accurate state. Even when that was done, the real anomalies remained.

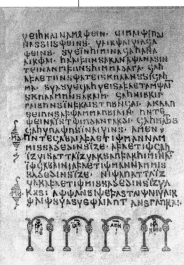

A Gospel
manuscript from
the late-antique
world, containing
the teachings
of Wulfila
(c. 311–383),
Codex Argentus,
handwritten in
the seventh
century.

The method of dealing with apparent contradictions, with obscure passages and with passages whose superficial meaning seemed unacceptable, was to look for different levels of meaning in the text. Medieval students of the Bible always approached it in the expectation that each

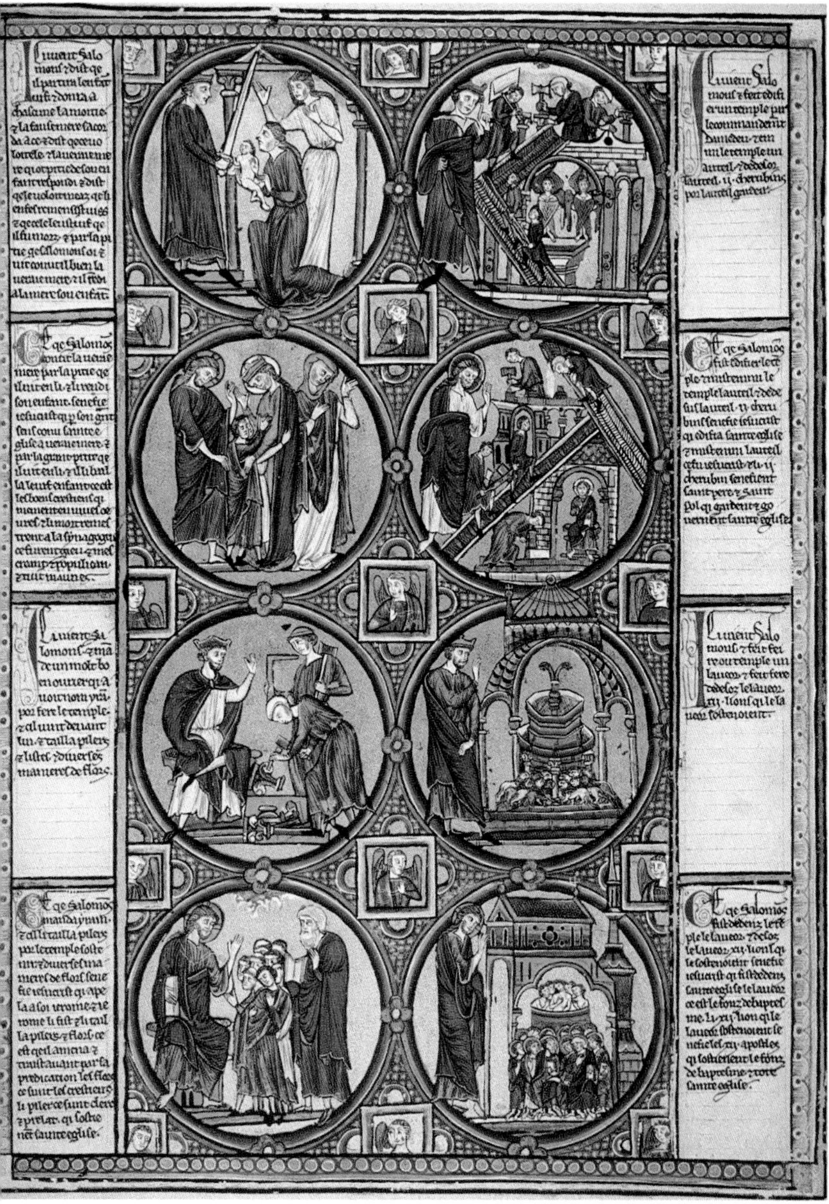

passage would have many meanings. Earlier students of
the Bible had done the same from early in the history of
Christianity, with the recognition from the beginning that
the books which were included in the canon were not
uniform in their approach.

The key idea was that the text had both a literal and a
figurative meaning. The literal meaning was simply 'what
the text seemed to be saying' on a straightforward reading.
(This was also called the 'historical' sense, but that can be
misleading because *historia* meant 'story'.) However, when
Christ was called 'the lion of Judah', no one thought that
this meant that he was literally a lion. The expression was
a metaphor, a 'transferred' usage. Similarly, talk of God
reaching out a 'strong right arm' could be taken to be an
image, and not literal. The great advantage of this division
into literal and figurative sense was that contradictions
could be made to disappear. A literal and a figurative
interpretation need not meet head on; one could slide
over the other.

There was the complication that the literal meaning
of the biblical text could itself be figurative. As an example,
when Jesus told his parables, he did not expect his readers
to take the stories to be factual. The woman who lost the
coin and searched hard to find it again, the wise virgins
who made sure they had oil in their lamps, and the sower
sowing his seed on different sorts of ground were clearly
tales with morals. This raised all sorts of difficulties for
biblical commentators in the Middle Ages. To them, it
meant that Jesus was, in a sense, not telling the truth
when he told these stories, because he was describing
things which had not happened.

There was a more positive reason for looking for
spiritual interpretations of biblical text than the 'emergency
solution' to the problem of the Bible's obscurities. An idea
which gained currency from the end of the second century
was that the figurative senses were higher and finer, more
spiritual, in the sense that they educated the soul more
profoundly than the literal senses.

This led to a need to determine the number and kind of such figurative 'senses'. As late as Augustine (354–430), this was still an extremely vexed question, and Augustine himself placed a surprising reliance on the book of rules of

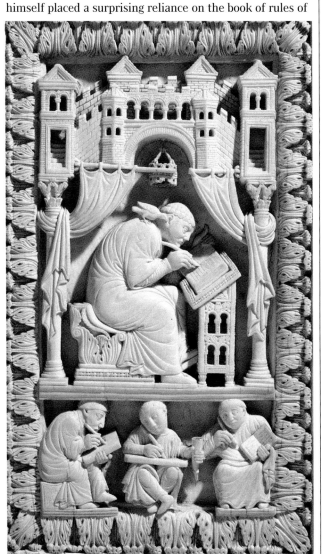

Pope Gregory the Great (590–604), scholar as well as Bishop of Rome, carved in a Carolingian ivory relief. The Holy Spirit in the form of a dove is guiding him as he writes, and below him are three scribes.

Tichonius. Tichonius belonged to a schismatic group called the Donatists and, therefore, in Augustine's eyes, he was an enemy to the true Church. However, there was no other convenient guidebook at the time.

Two centuries later, Pope Gregory the Great had developed a fourfold system of interpreting the Bible, which was to become standard throughout the medieval West. He began with the literal sense, and included three figurative senses. The first figurative sense was the 'allegorical' sense, where a word or story was to be taken to mean something in a transferred way. The lion of Judah is, again, a good example. The reader is expected to 'take' from the idea of a lion those elements which are appropriate to a comparison with Christ (royalty and nobility) and to leave out those which are not (yellowness, being four-footed).

The second figurative sense was the 'moral', or 'tropological', sense. Here, the interpreter pointed to the lessons to be learned from the passage of scripture about how to live a good Christian life. The most famous and widely read example of this kind of interpretation was Gregory's own *Moralia in Job*, a long and detailed analysis of the lessons about living a good Christian life which are to be learned from the book of Job.

The third figurative sense was the 'prophetic', or 'anagogical', sense. Here, the reader searched the text for indications of God's future intentions. Some commentators were especially attracted to this kind of analysis. At the beginning of the 12th century, the monastic scholar Rupert of Deutz created an immense framework for the whole of scripture and history. In it, the Old Testament represented the age of the Father and the New Testament represented the age of the Son. The age of the Holy Spirit stretched forward to the end of the world. Rupert was thus able to extend the comparison between figures in the Old and New Testaments into world history, and find analogies there.

A similar project, on a much smaller scale, was attempted by Anselm of Havelberg a decade or two later, when he wrote about God's providential purposes. Most notable of all, Joachim of Fiore interpreted from the Bible a symbolic system of threes and sevens. His attempts to move into the world of politics and to point a finger at the last world emperor made him the equivalent of today's 'sandwich-board man' in the last years of the 12th century – for he was, in effect, crying, 'The end of the world is at hand!' He caused enough anxiety in respectable circles in the Church to be condemned by the Fourth Lateran Council of 1215.

Nonetheless, the prophetic enterprise was not, in itself, disapproved of by the Church. Far from it; it had the potential to focus the minds of faithful Christians upon their end and to make them test all their activities against their hopes of heaven.

The Glossa Ordinaria

Perhaps the most practically useful achievement of the Middle Ages in terms of biblical interpretation was the creation of the *Glossa Ordinaria*. This was the drawing together of the older commentary material on the books of the Bible into a 'standard' commentary. Some books had always been more popular with preachers and commentators than others, so there were gaps to be filled. The work of assembling a complete commentary was done mainly during the 12th century, by a series of scholars, notable among whom was Anselm of Laon.

During the period 1230–35, when he was Regent Master in Paris, the Dominican Hugh of St Cher brought in material from the most recent scholarship in order to bring the *Glossa Ordinaria* up to date. He produced 'postils', or notes, on the whole of the Bible. These became, in their turn, a standard work of reference beyond the *Glossa Ordinaria*, acting as a supplement to it. Hugh of St Cher was born in about 1190 and ended his life in 1263 as a high-profile figure, a cardinal who had been Papal Legate to Germany (1251–53). He was the author of other works, in addition to his commentary on the Bible. His *Concordantia* of the whole Bible was still being reprinted in the 17th and 18th centuries. Even then, its orderly alphabetical arrangement of terms, by books and chapters of the Bible, made it both practical and accessible.

Early in the 14th century, another 'definitive' layer of commentary was added by the Franciscan Nicholas of Lyra (1270–1349). Lyra, who had some knowledge of Hebrew, completed a literal commentary on the entire Bible between 1322–23 and 1331. It was officially presented to Pope John XXII in 1331. Lyra intended it for the use of academic theologians, rather than for pastoral purposes.

This gradual accretion of 'layers' gave to the first printed Bibles the appearance of a set of concentric rings, or rather rectangles. A small square of biblical text was placed in the middle of the page and, around it, the *Glossa Ordinaria*, and these later additions and developments, working outwards.

Preaching the word

Preaching had, from the first, been one of the most important vehicles of biblical interpretation. Augustine

Bernard of Clairvaux

Bernard of Clairvaux (1090–1153) was another great preacher, who revived or continued the tradition of live preaching on scripture. He never became a bishop but, as Abbot of Clairvaux, he travelled and moved in diplomatic as well as in ecclesiastical circles, and he had great influence. He made an intimate use of scripture in his sermons. In his long series of sermons on the Song of Songs, for example, he comes to the passage, 'My beloved is mine and I am his.' Bernard says, 'It is the Bridegroom whose words we have pondered until now. We implore his presence that we may worthily trace the words of his Bride, to his glory and for our salvation. For we cannot worthily consider and study such words as these unless he is present to guide our discourse. For her words are pleasant and lovely, bringing profit to the understanding, and they are deep in mystery.'

Pope Innocent III
approves the
preaching 'order'
of friars founded
by Francis of
Assisi.
Fresco by Giotto
di Bondone.

and Gregory the Great both saw the bishop as a teacher. The *cathedra*, or seat from which the bishop taught, gives its very name to a 'cathedral'. Both Augustine and Gregory were highly successful preachers, who could hold a large audience for hours, in the noisy style favoured at the time, where the congregation would applaud a sermon they particularly enjoyed. Augustine preached long series of sermons, for example, his 'Narrations on the Psalms'. Gregory did so, too, in his sermons on the book of Ezekiel. For some centuries after Gregory the Great, live preaching became less usual, but sermons on books of scripture, which dated from the earlier centuries, were still read.

Preaching the word began to appear in a slightly different light in the later Middle Ages, with an increasing separation of the ministry of the word and the ministry of

'While brother John of Penna was still a boy... a beautiful child appeared to him one night [and told him to go and listen to a friar who was preaching locally]. And he went to St Stephen's, and found a large crowd of men and women gathered there to hear the sermon... Then brother Philip stood up to preach, and spoke with the greatest devotion, proclaiming the kingdom of everlasting life not with words of human wisdom but with the power of the Spirit.'

FRANCIS OF ASSISI
(1181–1226), *THE
LITTLE FLOWERS OF
ST FRANCIS*

the sacraments. The founding of the mendicant orders of preaching friars, the Dominicans and the Franciscans, meant that, from the early 13th century, there were 'specialists' in preaching.

Meanwhile, the sacramental ministry, especially the saying of the Mass, tended to become something separate, with the focus on the action of the priest. In chapter 10, we shall see the problems that this caused in Western Christendom.

Sermons in Latin on the Latin text of scripture were, in any case, an unsatisfactory way of bringing God's word to people who did not speak Latin. It is a puzzle that there is little surviving evidence of what went into sermons preached to the people in their own language. Those preachers who preserved their sermons tended to do so in the Latin version. Especially in the growing and prosperous towns of the later Middle Ages, people began to clamour for something they could use and understand.

Attempts at vernacular translations of the Bible were one symptom of this new need. Another was the return to an emphasis on the ministry of the word as a central part of the work of a priest, which was to be one of the great driving forces of the Reformation.

Defining the Church

If the Bible was the inspired word of God, what else did Christians need? Another way of putting this question is to ask: What was left to be completed after the resurrection of Christ? For even if Christ had paid the penalty for sin, that self-evidently did not mean that all those who had faith in him ceased to commit sins. There was obviously a great deal more to do, and by the early Middle Ages it was held that it was the task of the Church, which Jesus himself had founded, to do it (Matthew 16:18).

'Church' meant the buildings in which people met to worship, which grew more and more splendid as the Middle Ages wore on and they were built 'to the glory of God'. However, it also had deeper meanings, which were less easy to portray. Above all, the Church was the community of the faithful.

The Church as community

The person who becomes a Christian also becomes a member of a community. In the first Christian centuries, the emphasis was on the local 'churches', where people formed small groups. Far from having handsome buildings, they were often forced to live and worship in secret because of the periodical persecution of Christians by the state. When Paul wrote the 'letters' to the Colossians, the Ephesians and the Philippians – which survive in the New Testament – he was addressing such communities, at Colossus, Ephesus and Philippi. He warned them about the infighting which was hard to avoid in their closed-in small communities. However, it was also obvious from an early stage that it was going to be necessary to create a bigger organization or structure, if Christians were not to split up into warring factions, and if there was to be a sensible protection against 'charismatic' leaders with ideas of their own, who might lead people off into sects and divisions.

One major division in the early Christian community was between those who had formerly been Jews and those who had come from other races. Christians worshipped the God of the Jews, but with a new understanding of his intentions for humanity. It was, therefore, difficult for former Jews to know how much of their old observance they should be required to keep to.

In chapter 15 of the Acts of the Apostles, there is a description of an episode in which Christians from Judea were teaching the faithful that they must follow the old Jewish rules and submit to circumcision. Paul and Barnabas argued with them but could not persuade them. So it was decided that they should all go to Jerusalem to discuss the matter with the 'apostles and elders'. There, the argument continued, until Peter got up and addressed the meeting. He reminded them that it had been agreed that

A small medieval church at Whitby in the north of England caters for a community's needs.

By contrast, the majesty of Chartres Cathedral shows the wealth and power of the Church.

he should be 'apostle to the Gentiles', and he said that it was his experience that God converted non-Jews just as he did Jews, making no difference between them. Why, then, he argued, impose a yoke on their necks by making them observe Jewish rituals? He was supported by the apostle James. It was decided to write a moderate letter to the Christians in Antioch, Syria and Cilicia, where this was a matter of particular dispute. In the letter, they were encouraged to keep clear of idolatry and fornication, as the Jews did, but told that they were not expected to take on the whole burden of Jewish observance now that they were Christians.

This was not the end of dispute, by any means. The same chapter of the Acts of the Apostles describes how Paul quarrelled with Barnabas, and how each took a different companion before going off in opposite directions to preach. But it did suggest a way in which Christians could resolve differences and arrive at common decisions on points of faith and order. This method, of holding a 'council', became established. A series of general or 'ecumenical' councils was held in the first centuries, at which the Holy Spirit was believed to be present. At each, the assembled leaders of the Church formally ratified the decisions of those who had been at the previous council and declared themselves to be unanimous, thus preserving a continuity in 'the mind of the Church'.

This raised other questions, about the authority of the leaders to decide 'for' the community, and how that was to be balanced against the right of the whole community to have its say. The community developed both patterns of leadership, and a recognition that Christians had a collective 'mind' and could form a consensus – the *consensus fidelium*, or 'agreement of the faithful'. There was always a tension between this strikingly modern and rather 'democratic' idea and the evolving formal leadership. The one thing almost everyone was able to accept was that there must be no division about the faith. There must be 'one faith' uniting Christians.

'If any of you have a dispute with another Christian, how dare you go before heathen judges instead of letting God's people settle the matter?... Surely there is at least one wise person in your fellowship who can settle a dispute between fellow-Christians.'

1 CORINTHIANS 6:1, 5

In the early Christian world there was another phenomenon which caused problems. Jesus had told his disciples to go out and preach and win disciples. That was what they did. But without centralized organization, such wandering preaching sometimes threw up wild, charismatic figures, whose teaching was not easy to control – people who claimed that they were 'led by the Spirit' and were, in effect, appealing to a direct divine mandate. Another debate of the early Church was, therefore, about the balance between 'charism' and 'order'. Requiring those who spoke for the Church to be given some sort of mandate was the natural response of officialdom in the Church to the threat posed by letting people say what they liked in the name of Christ.

'I saw [bishops] living in London... Some took posts at Court counting the Kings' money... Others went into the service of lords and ladies, sitting like stewards managing household affairs... I fear that there are many whom Christ... will curse for ever.'

WILLIAM
LANGLAND,
PIERS PLOWMAN,
MID-14TH CENTURY

Ministers of the Church

The New Testament describes a variety of types of ministers: 'elders', 'apostles' and also 'deacons'. The deacons are the category whose functions we can be most sure of. They were the people who looked after the widows and orphans, and did practical good work. The others, 'elders', 'apostles' and so on, were the leaders who were also teachers, and who united the community 'under' them, with the apostles naturally the most respected in the first generation, because they had actually known Jesus.

By the Middle Ages these shadowy early forms of ministry, about whose exact nature there is a great deal of modern scholarly debate, had become fixed. Eventually, certainly by the early medieval period, there was a ladder. There was ordination first to the diaconate (the office of deacon), then to the priesthood and then to the episcopate (the office of bishop). A deacon could not say the Mass. Only a priest or a bishop was able to declare forgiveness when a penitent confessed. Only a bishop could ordain new priests.

In the West, monks were not necessarily ordained, and their 'hierarchy' should not be confused with that of the deacons, priests and bishops. Monks in Benedictine houses had abbots, usually of the higher social classes, who were the targets of satire, just like the wealthy bishops, like Chaucer's 'hunting, shooting and fishing' monk. Though they might see bishops (and abbots) passing on fine horses (and there was a good deal of critical comment about that), most people did not have much to do with the higher reaches of this clerical hierarchy in the Middle Ages.

In ordinary people's lives in the later Middle Ages, the ministry was likely to be represented by the local parish priest. Chaucer's 'Poor Parson of a Town', from his *Canterbury Tales*, was a learned man, a clerk, 'that Christ's gospel truly would preach; his parishioners devoutly would he teach'. He was patient in adversity and charitable to his parishioners.

The responsibilities of a parish priest were pastoral. The parishioners' children had to be baptized, and there were marriages to be celebrated. But above all, from at least the 12th century, there was a penitential role.

A small child 'oblate' is 'given' to a monastery to be a monk, with a fee changing hands.
From *Decretium* by Gratian.

Confession

The defining moment in the evolution of the sacrament of penance in the Middle Ages was the requirement of the Fourth Lateran Council of 1215 that everyone, of either sex, should confess to a priest at least once a year, in Lent. But well before that, and leading up to it, had come a natural development of penitential practice in response to pastoral need. Baptism was believed to wipe away all original and actual sin completely. When everyone was baptized in infancy, it was inevitable that a catalogue of actual sins would follow. Yet baptism could not be repeated. It was

'Well ought a priest ensample for to give; By his cleanness, how that his sheep should live.'

CHAUCER,
CANTERBURY TALES,
PROLOGUE (1387–88)

held firmly, from the earliest days of the Church, that a person could be baptized only once. The reason for this was Christ's saying that someone who put his hand to the plough and looked back was not fit for the kingdom of heaven (Luke 9:62).

In some 'rigorist' early communities, those who sinned after baptism were cast out for ever. Others allowed penitents to return, but only after a considerable period of public penance, during which they were dressed in special clothing and separated from the rest of the congregation. This 'public penance' was usually imposed for serious sins, such as murder, adultery or apostasy (renunciation of faith), and the restoration to the community required the bishop to declare the penitent forgiven.

During the early Middle Ages, it was realized that this was not going to meet everyone's ordinary needs for cleansing from more everyday sins, and the practice grew of confessing privately, not to the bishop, but to a priest. This created a need for instruction manuals for priests, so that they could judge fairly what penalties it was appropriate to impose for particular sins. It was accepted that something more was required than merely to admit the sin and repent of it. The priest should expect the penitent to demonstrate the sincerity of the repentance by some action, such as almsgiving or fasting.

None of this penitential practice affected the work of a parish priest directly, but it did so indirectly, partly because it made for immense complications in the Christian lives of

Marriage was both a sacrament and a social occasion. A medieval wedding-scene by the Master of the Jarves Cassoni, illustrating The Story of Alatiel in the *Decameron* by Boccaccio.

Opposite page:
The portrait of
the Pardoner
from the
'Ellesmere'
Chaucer
(1400–10).

Indulgences

An indulgence was not part of the penitential system, but it depended on that underlying structure of assumptions. An indulgence was the remission by the Church of the temporal penalty of forgiven sin (the punishment imposed by a priest, not the eternal consequences). So, it was a 'letting off' of the acts which would otherwise have had to be done in penance. The idea was that God recognized the Church's 'sentences' on penitents, because he had given the Church authority to impose them. This was based on Jesus' grant of the power to bind and loose in heaven and on earth, which came to be known as 'the power of the keys' – that is, the power to use, or refuse to use, the 'keys' to let someone into heaven (Matthew 16:19 and 18:18). It was expected that God would require penances to be discharged before the person on whom they were imposed could be admitted to heaven.

A pope selling indulgences in a woodcut from 1521 by Lucas Cranach the Elder.

The Church – this required a bishop or the pope himself – could relax these penalties. Pope Urban II did this when he granted a 'plenary indulgence' (that is, a remission of all their penances and direct entry into heaven) to those who went on the First Crusade and either died on the way or got as far as Jerusalem. In the course of the later Middle Ages, it occurred to the Church's authorities that they could charge money for indulgences, and the system became corrupted, with anxious relatives trying to buy freedom from the penitential burden for those who had died.

the population. It bred anxiety and a sense that it was necessary to work extremely hard to earn a place in heaven. One of its most visible effects was to give a disproportionate prominence to the importance of 'saying Masses'. It was held that saying a Mass could 'apply' the effects of the sacrifice of Christ – that is, his death on the cross – to the spiritual needs of individuals. The emphasis moved, therefore, from the participation of the faithful in the eucharist, or holy communion, because these Masses could be said by a priest alone, and pious laypeople might pay for a certain number of Masses to be said for them for a particular purpose.

Preaching or teaching his parishioners (the ministry of the word) was the other main part of a parish priest's duties, but the effect of the concentration on the 'sacrificial' aspect of the eucharist or Mass was often to diminish, or almost eliminate, the ministry of the word. In any case, simple homilies about how to be a good Christian were all an unlearned priest might manage. The level of education of the parish priest was usually not high. Because of the 'ignorance of priests', Archbishop Pecham held a provincial Council at Lambeth in 1281, at which a plan of 'instruction for the laity' was drawn up. This was turned into verse for use in the province of York in 1357, on the orders of Archbishop Thoresby. An indulgence of 40 days was given with it, to encourage people to learn it and teach it to other people. It was still in Latin, however, though in 1425 it was translated into English at the instigation of the Bishop of Bath and Wells. He had it put in every church in the diocese, and he told his archdeacons to sell all the clergy copies at sixpence each. These are striking advances, but they are patchy and spaced over a considerable period of time, and they do not suggest that the clergy generally were always delivering a very high standard of pastoral ministry.

Really good, sophisticated preaching with a sound theological basis needed an expertise and education which few parish priests had. From the 13th century, there were 'experts' about, who could deliver powerful, exciting

'There was also a Pardoner… He produced a document covered with bishops' seals, and claimed to have power to absolve all the people… The ignorant folk believed him and were delighted. They came up and knelt to kiss his documents while he… raked in their rings and jewellery with his roll of parchment.'

WILLIAM LANGLAND, *PIERS PLOWMAN,* MID-14TH CENTURY

sermons to stir people up to stronger faith and deeper understanding. These were the friars, whom we shall meet in a later chapter.

The medieval papacy

Jesus said to Peter that Peter was the rock on which Jesus would build his Church (Matthew 16:18). Already in the period after the end of the Roman empire, there was debate about which of the ancient patriarchates was the most senior. Pope Gregory I (Gregory the Great) was one of the main protagonists of the argument that Rome should come first. In the late 11th century, Pope Gregory VII began to enlarge the claims of the papacy, not only over against the other leaders of the Church – including the bishops of the West – but also in relation to the state.

A document known as the *Donation of Constantine* was relied upon for much of the Middle Ages, although it eventually turned out to be an early forgery. It suggested that the first Christian emperor, Constantine, had, as a gesture, 'given' authority over the state to the Church. Gregory VII strengthened that position, claiming that 'at the knee of the pope every king should bow'.

This was a period in which Church and state were engaged in a dispute known as the Investiture Contest.

A handbook for priests

There are indications that the Church was sufficiently concerned to try to educate the parish clergy better, which is in itself an indication that there was a problem. William of Pagula wrote an *Oculus sacerdotis*, or 'Priest's Eye', in the early 14th century. It was an immensely practical handbook, divided into three sections. In the first, the priest was told how to hear confessions. This included suggesting what questions to ask in order to ascertain which of the seven deadly sins his penitents had committed, so that priest and penitent alike should have a clear framework. The second section gave the priest help with catechesis and the general instruction of laypeople in the way to live a good Christian life. The last part was full of resource material for the priest on theological and sacramental matters. This was only one of a considerable number of such works in use in the last medieval centuries.

Every time a bishop died and had to be replaced, there was a complex process in which the local king or emperor handed over the lands of the diocese (the 'temporalities') and the Church consecrated the new bishop for his office (the 'spiritualities'). Royal patrons had been intruding on the Church's part of this process, giving the new bishop his pastoral staff or the ring which symbolized his 'marriage' to his diocese. This dispute reached an uneasy settlement in the Concordat of Worms of 1122, but it prompted still more determined self-aggrandisement on the part of the Church. Bernard of Clairvaux wrote a series of letters to Pope Eugenius III, called *On Consideration*, in which he spelled out for the pope the position in the universe which set him above everything on earth.

The consequences of this rebalancing of the powers of Church and state, and of the pope within the Church, were enormous. The following medieval centuries saw a growing papal monarchy, and less and less awareness of the Church as a community.

One of the great medieval difficulties was to keep the live and individual experience of a personal faith in Christ in balance with the enormous growth of the institutional structure of the Church, which was associated with the rise of the papacy to such a position of monarchical power. That was, perhaps, the chief development of Christianity in the Middle Ages; it was certainly the most conspicuous. It set up tensions which led, in the end, to a lasting division of the faithful from the period of the Reformation of the 16th century.

Laypeople

I n a hierarchical society, in which the social strata were 'fixed', most educated people were likely to be from the classes whose members were at least free and not in poverty. The educated in the Middle Ages were mostly the clergy. The word 'cleric' and the word 'clerk' come from the same source, and a priest was for a long time known in English as a 'clerk in holy orders'. These two social and educational factors encouraged a division in most people's thinking between those who ran the Church and the bulk of those who made it up.

The people of God, the *laos*, were really the whole 'people', including the clergy. However, that sense of the term was easily lost sight of, with clergy and people alike falling into the habit of thinking that only the ordinary people were the 'laity'.

In these circumstances, there was a natural tendency for theologians, and the Church's own hierarchy, to regard laypeople as 'children' in the faith, and to expect less of them theologically. This was reinforced by the gulf which opened up after the end of the Roman world between those who knew Latin and those who spoke only the local vernacular. Several of those vernacular languages – Italian, Spanish and French – remained close to Latin for some centuries, and it is not easy to say when they ceased to be Latin and became new languages. If people could not read, they were largely cut off from the finer points of what was written, in any case.

How far could laypeople be expected to understand the subtleties of the faith, where the arguments and the teaching were being conducted in Latin? The answers to that question are sometimes surprising. In the 12th century, there arose groups known as the 'Poor Men of Lyons', led by a man called Waldes, or Valdez. They were also called the

A late-medieval cloth market in the Netherlands, showing a busy trading life in a lively community.

'Waldensians', after this leader. They questioned the role of the clergy as they knew it. There was a mounting resentment of the claims that no one could get to heaven without the assistance of the Church, when some of its leading ministers were manifestly taking advantage of their position to swagger about in fine clothes on expensive horses, and leaving the pastoral care of their people to curates.

The Waldensians belonged to the early 'middle classes'. They were townspeople, tradesmen, people of enterprise, who set about gaining an understanding of what was in the Bible by reading it for themselves. Theologically, they were not unorthodox, except in this one respect of their challenge to the need to rely on the Church for one's salvation. When attempts were made by the Church's apologists to bring them to order by quoting scripture at them, they answered smartly back, using their own quotations.

The same practical method of self-help was adopted in the late 14th century by followers of John Wyclif, who were known as the Lollards. Surprisingly sophisticated Bible study was going on in Lollard 'house-groups' in the 15th century, with the same idea that ordinary people ought to be able to learn about their faith.

But oh, to see the Church so split
Should cover all of us with gloom…
Consider now the latest sprout
Which pride and envy have made grow
From schism, and to which we owe
This recent sect of Lollardy.

JOHN GOWER, *CONFESSIO AMANTIS*, MID-14TH CENTURY

John Gower was born in about 1330, of a solid country family which gave him enough social standing to gain an entry to court circles. He was an enemy of the Lollards, but he himself, writing within a different framework of conventions, exemplified some of the understanding of the issues of faith which the Lollards also demonstrated. Like the Lollards, Gower showed that ordinary laypeople were not necessarily as ignorant of theology as the clergy sometimes liked to think. He wrote books in three languages, *The Voice of One Crying* in Latin, *The Mirror of One Meditating* in French, and *The Confession of Love* in English.

In *The Confession of Love*, Gower uses the device of getting Venus to appoint her chaplain to hear Gower confess his sins. The chaplain sets out the catalogue of the seven deadly sins. He looks at them first from a Christian point of view and then from the satirical point of view of an adherent of courtly love. Courtly love was an artificial game of 'pretend' courting of an inaccessible highly born married lady, which was a fashion of the day. One of the questions Gower raises with his confessor is whether a Christian is allowed to kill. No, God forbids it, says the confessor, and gives a little homily on the virtues of peace:

And when his Son was born, he sent
  Down angels, through the firmament,
Whose song of peace the shepherds heard.

JOHN GOWER, *CONFESSIO AMANTIS*, MID-14TH CENTURY

Julian of Norwich is an example of a female mystic of the later Middle Ages, who was both formed and limited by certain expectations of the laity. She can have had limited formal education, but both female and male laypeople sometimes had the opportunity to discuss religious beliefs and perceptions with Dominican and Franciscan friars who came to preach locally. In 1373, Julian had a series of visions, which she called 'showings'. She reflected on these for two decades, and then, in the 1390s, she wrote her *Revelation of Divine Love*. The writing, like the experience, is vivid. 'I saw the bodily sight of the dying Christ,' she claims. She describes 'the plenteous bleeding of the head' and the way 'the great drops of blood fell down from under the garland'.

The reputation of such a mystic could spread through tales of her wonderful experiences, and also through reading her writings. Julian was visited in Norwich by Margery Kemp,

Hildegard of Bingen and Mechthild of Magdeburg

Hildegard of Bingen (1098–1179) was a child who had visions. In 1141, she reported that she had been given a knowledge of scripture which others achieved only by patient reading. Ten years' work followed, at the end of which she had completed her *Scivias*. In about 1158, Hildegard began to travel on preaching journeys. The Lollard women preachers had not yet made an 'issue' of women engaging in this kind of ministry. Hildegard delivered apocalyptic sermons at Cologne and Trier. Hers was not a call for radical reform; nor was it millennarianism. Nevertheless, in her old age, Hildegard became something of a controversial figure.

Hildegard of Bingen and some of her visions. Manuscript illustration (c. 1230).

A 14th-century female figure who invited comparison with Hildegard was Mechthild of Magdeburg. She lived in community for a time, as a Beguine. These were groups of women (though groups of men were formed, too) who lived together, caring for the poor and sick, without taking the formal vows of a nun. She, too, had visions, which she wrote about in Low German. Mechthild's themes are of the overflowing of the Godhead upon creation, and of the love which was the essence of that outflowing.

Like Hildegard of Bingen, Mechthild grew bold. She became a critic and social commentator. She won both admiration and opprobrium. She had the spiritual counsel of a Dominican friar, Heinrich of Halle, who was a pupil of Albert the Great, Thomas Aquinas' teacher. That helped to bring her into the mainstream. With the assistance of Dominicans, collections of such writing began to be disseminated in 14th-century Germany. Lay spirituality, especially that of women, could become associated with social comment in this way, partly because of its association with the active work of the friars among the people.

whose own book, *The Book of Margery Kemp*, is another example of this type of lay female writing. Margery herself certainly had opportunities to hear Dominicans preaching in local pulpits.

It was possible for popular religious movements to remain 'within the fold', but it was not easy. The establishment tended to regard them with suspicion precisely because the laity was not under obedience in the same way as were members of conventional religious orders, or priests (who owed canonical obedience to their bishops). In other words, there were fears that they would get out of control. Among the popular movements which preserved a degree of 'respectability' were the 'third orders' of friars, who formed the 'confraternities' of the 13th century. These associations had the authority of the bishop, and their members were bound together by rules. The Flagellants were a more dangerous manifestation, because of their inherently 'extreme' common interests. They would march naked through the streets, bewailing their sins and encouraging public confession of sins and crimes. This was an Italian movement in origin, although it spread some distance across Europe in the course of the 13th century before it subsided. In 12th-century Italy, 'singing gilds' arose,

Flagellants from the 14th century walking through the streets behind the sign of the cross and beating themselves. Illustration from the *Chronicles of Aegidius*.

which evolved into more formal organizations with chapels.
They held processions and met in piazzas and sang hymns in
vernacular languages.

Not all the ordinary laity took such an intellectual,
spiritual or energetic interest in their faith. Many were
content, and were encouraged to be content, with 'pictures'
on the church wall.

Popular piety

The cult of the Blessed Virgin Mary flourished in the West
from the 12th century. It was not that there had not been
reverence for Mary earlier than this, especially in the East.
But a series of Western writers now drew attention to her, and
encouraged Christians to focus their thoughts and prayers
upon her. Anselm of Canterbury wrote a prayer to Mary in the
new tradition of personal private prayer which he encouraged.

Bernard of Clairvaux played a part in the reform of the
Cistercian liturgy, which helped to bring to prominence the
act of worship associated with the relatively new Feast of
the Assumption of the Virgin (the belief that Jesus' mother
Mary did not die in the ordinary way, but was taken up into
heaven at the end of her life). In the Cistercian form of
service, there is a strong association of Mary with the Song
of Songs. In the form of worship ('office") for the Nativity of
the Virgin there is an antiphon, 'Behold you are beautiful my
love, behold you are beautiful. Your eyes are doves…'; and
another at Vespers, 'You are most beautiful, my beloved…
come and you shall be crowned.'

A 'cult' of the Virgin developed, which had a strong
popular attraction. Mary was a figure to whom ordinary
people could 'relate'. It was easy to pray to her to ask her
to intercede with her Son, Jesus.

There was also a strengthening in the medieval West of
the cult of the saints, which was always a powerful element
in popular religion in the East. In the East, it had long been
customary to revere the very 'icons' of the saints, to a
degree where, in the eighth and ninth centuries, there
was a period of active controversy, in which one party (the

'Iconoclasts') pressed for the destruction of these icons. In Byzantine churches, medieval and more recent icons can still be seen, hung with votive tablets. These show, for example, an eye, an arm or a leg, hung there by the faithful in the hope of a cure for an ailment.

The Western controversy about this came much later, at the very end of the Middle Ages. At this time, the reverence of ordinary people, not only for pictures and statues of saints, but also for 'relics', such as fingernails, bones and the hair of saints, began to seem to some critics rather like idolatry. There was a fine line between asking God to help for the sake of the goodness of his saint and attributing to the saints themselves, or to physical objects associated with them, semi-divine powers close to magic. It was expecting a great deal to hope that ordinary people would stay on the right side of this line and not become confused, and reformers began to express serious concerns as the Middle Ages came to an end.

Christian goodness for ordinary people

What was a good person? In his book, *The Perfect Righteousness of Man*, Augustine had come to the conclusion that there was only one good man – Jesus himself. For ordinary people, there was no hope of being truly good. Augustine wanted to emphasize the need for God's help ('grace'). Some medieval thinkers, such as Peter Abelard, went so far as to argue that the main purpose of Christ's coming was to show what man was created to be.

There was a dilemma here. On the one hand, the Church's teachers wanted to encourage people to trust in God and to rely on him as their only means of rescue from sin. On the other hand, they wanted people to strive to be good. This balance between 'faith' and 'works' was to become important in the last medieval phase, when reformers began to complain that the Church had allowed – even encouraged – a 'pastoral drift' towards an emphasis on 'good works' and 'earning your way to heaven'. Like the questions about the excessive devotion to the saints, this became one of the 'Church-dividing' issues which brought the Middle Ages to a close.

The 'assumption' or ascent into heaven of Mary the mother of Jesus. The belief that she ascended bodily in this way on her death began from about the fourth century. Since the sixth century the feast in celebration of her assumption has been on 15 August and is still important in the Orthodox and Roman Catholic calendars. *The Assumption of the Virgin Mary* by Sano di Pietro.

CHAPTER 6

Politics and the Church

The earliest Christians often came from the lowlier parts of society, and some were slaves. The Christian religion was, at first, a minority religion, of which the state disapproved. From time to time in the first Christian centuries, there was active persecution against Christians. All that changed when the emperor Constantine himself became a Christian in the early fourth century, and the Roman empire adopted Christianity as the 'state' religion. His 'conversion' was probably as much political as religious. He wanted to win a battle, and he thought that the cross of Christ might be the 'sign' under which he would conquer. Symbolic of Constantine's attitude to his new faith was the fact that he built a ring of Christian churches around the edge of Rome, leaving the pagan temples of the inner city untouched.

The transformation of old pagan temples into Christian churches ought to be a useful indicator of the degree of penetration of Christianity into the pagan Roman world. It was more common in the East than in the West, but in Rome the Pantheon was converted to a church in the seventh century. Yet the evidence is not easy to interpret. Many ancient temples were excavated in the past by classical archaeologists who were not looking for Christian remains and did not preserve what they found, so it is hard to be sure that evidence was not destroyed. To build a Christian church on the site of a temple as soon as the temple was abandoned made a statement. But to use a convenient platform, two centuries later, when the

Roman sculpture of Constantine the Great, the first Christian emperor.

local people had half-forgotten what the temple had stood for, shows only that public observance of the old religion had ceased. Between the fifth and the seventh centuries, much changed in the world of Western Europe. There seems to have been some lingering sense of the grandeur of the old buildings, and it was not unknown for a temple façade to be preserved so as to maintain a fine vista, even when the temple behind had vanished.

This uncertainty about the 'temple-to-church' transformation reflects a similar difficulty in being sure how far Christianity had really penetrated into ordinary people's lives and minds at the beginning of the medieval period. Augustine of Hippo's mother seems to have maintained a simple peasant's reverence for the shrines of the saints that was little different from the old worship of the gods, and she was far from untypical. It was not unusual for someone who had become a Christian to go on being a pagan, too – just to be on the safe side.

Citizens (or subjects) have to live in a community and under its laws. This recognition was central to Christianity from the beginning. Jesus was asked whether it was right

The Pantheon, a Roman temple which was turned into a Christian church in the seventh century.

to pay taxes (Matthew 22:15–22). He asked to be shown a coin, and then asked whose head appeared on it. 'Pay the Emperor what belongs to the Emperor,' he said. So, the Christian was to keep a separation in his loyalties between his duty to God and his 'civic' duty, but he was also to be an obedient citizen. There was a similar theme in the advice of the apostle Paul (Ephesians 6:5) that slaves should obey their masters. Christians were not social revolutionaries in any active sense, revolutionary though their ideas were in their potential for changing society from the inside. The only note of violent disagreement with society's norms was struck by Jesus himself, when he threw the money-changers out of the Temple in Jerusalem (Matthew 21:12). He was objecting to the intrusion of secular values into the place where God was to be worshipped. There was sufficient potential 'nuance' in these passages to afford many centuries of debate in the Christian West about the balance which ought to be struck by a faithful Christian between his duty to God and his duty to the state.

In his *The City of God*, Augustine of Hippo brought things up to date for Christians at the end of the ancient world. He emphasized that the 'city' of which Christians are citizens is eternal. It is God's City. Its members include people who have already died and people not yet born. Similarly 'eternal' is the 'other' city, made up of those who are not God's people. Looking around the faces to be seen in this life, one may not know who belongs to which city. Asking whether they belong to the Church is not a reliable way to tell. They may be regular churchgoers and still not be among God's 'chosen'. Only God knows who are his own. Even the individual himself does not know. This way of thinking encourages citizens to look towards the next world.

There is a further complication, in that the idea of the 'state' did not always have its modern connotations. The way it was envisaged depended on the structures of government involved, and also on an ideology. In the late

A king listening to the Church's advice. This was really rather rare. Royal patronage could make sure that bishops were often beholden to the state for their positions in the Middle Ages. From *Codex Sophilogium*.

Roman period, the head of state was an emperor, and there arose a cult of the emperor himself. Good citizens were expected to 'worship' him.

Because the transition to the Middle Ages involved the collapse of the old Roman political and social structures, there were immense and radical changes in the patterns of life for ordinary people and also for their leaders. Augustine's broad, and essentially other-worldly, picture made it easier to carry over Christian ideals of a 'heavenly' citizenship – where the citizen's first loyalties were to God – through centuries of change, upheaval and reconstruction, leading to the development of the feudal system in Northern Europe and big changes to the old city states in Italy.

This kind of event is a useful reminder that religion always has a place in society. For the Middle Ages, the social and political role of Christianity was to be central. In medieval Europe, a nominal 'Holy' Roman empire persisted, but the dominant pattern in most of Northern Europe was the feudal system, with a royal figure at its head.

The 'king' became idealized, not because anyone who had dealings with actual kings had any illusions about the royal realities, but because he retained, with appropriate Christian modifications, something of the aura of semi-

The French king
Philip IV
(1268–1314) with
senior clerics and
nobles at a
council meeting.
From *Grandes
Chroniques de
France*.

divinity which used to be attached to the Roman emperor. In the Christian version, the king was 'anointed' by God, rather than being 'divine' himself. This did not give him priestly powers or functions. It was always clear that a Christian king was not a 'priest-king'. But it did make him God's 'favourite', and the recipient of a divine 'authority to rule'. There was a good deal of self-consciousness about the importance of this distinction. That assumption is reflected in the coronation ceremonies in which the Church 'made' the king the legitimate vessel of an authority which comes from God.

At a more modest and human level, all this made it

important that a king should be seen to be a good Christian, to set a religious example as the leading layman. Kings are praised in medieval narratives for their piety, as well as for their courage and competence on the battlefield.

Conflicts of loyalty

In feudalism, a king owns the lands of his kingdom and he allows his 'vassals' to 'hold' portions of his lands at his pleasure. In return for the lands, the vassals swear an oath of allegiance to their king, kneeling and placing their hands between his. In their turn, these vassals become the 'barons' of the kingdom. They owe the king so many days of knight-service a year; in other words, they have to find him soldiers to serve in his armies. Their own people work on their lands as farmers, in a further relationship of subservience. These serfs might, in some circumstances, hope to be emancipated, but room for 'social mobility' is extremely limited in a feudal environment.

This had various implications for Christians, as well as for the Church and its institutions. Land could not be 'held' outside the feudal system. So churches and especially bishoprics and also monasteries, which all needed lands, held land of the king, like everyone else. In return they, too, had to provide their days of 'knight-service' and other feudal dues. Bishops were, in effect, barons themselves, and that was, to some degree, also true of abbots. When kings granted charters, the barons who were present would attach their names, and the names of bishops and abbots appeared alongside those of secular lords. In fact, they came first in the order of precedence because they were spiritual, not secular, lords. So, this was a society in which the leaders of the Church had a clearly defined 'place' in the secular world, and also certain duties there.

There were, naturally, conflicts of loyalty. Anselm, Archbishop of Canterbury in 1092–1109, went into exile twice, seeking support from the pope, because of problems with two successive kings of England, William II and

'This world is chiefly ruled by the sacred authority of bishops and the power of kings... But the episcopal dignity is greater than the royal, for bishops consecrate kings, but kings do not consecrate bishops.'

HINCMAR OF
RHEIMS (c. 806–82)

'The Prince is the public power, and an image of God's majesty on earth... For all power is from God... Whatever the Prince has power to do comes from God.'

JOHN OF SALISBURY,
POLICRATICUS,
MID-12TH CENTURY

Henry I. On the first occasion he found himself in conflict with the king, it was over exactly this question of where his first loyalty lay. This was one of the numerous periods when there were rival candidates for the papacy, and Anselm had given his loyalty to Urban II before he became archbishop. For political reasons, William II favoured Urban's rival, and he did not want his Archbishop of Canterbury on the opposite side. Anselm could not bring himself to abandon his honest commitment. To whom did he owe obedience? He believed it was to Urban; the king said it was to him, as feudal overlord.

The whole question had become even more complicated at this time, because kings and emperors had fallen into the habit of 'investing' new bishops with the ring and staff of their office. It took three principal steps to make a bishop. First, a name had to be chosen. That was, in theory, a matter for the people of the diocese, but it had, in practice, long been accepted that it lay with kings to nominate candidates. Family connections could be important. Bishops could function as barons best if they were the brothers and cousins of other barons and came from the same noble families. Then the king or emperor invested the new bishop with the lands or 'temporalities' of the diocese. And the Church performed its quite distinct 'sacramental' part, in which the secular authorities had no role. This was what made the bishop into a bishop. The 'investment' with the ring and the staff were tokens of this part of the making of a bishop. The ring symbolized the marriage of the bishop with the people of his diocese; the pastoral staff his role as their shepherd.

When Anselm of Canterbury was made archbishop, he had been reluctant to accept the office which was being (literally) thrust upon him with these symbols. It was a convention from the earliest Christian centuries that new bishops should pretend that they were unwilling to be given high office in this way. But in Anselm's case it was genuine enough. This meant that he had, in fact, resisted the 'investment' with the ring and staff which the king (who had no authority) had attempted to perform in person. In later years, when he had a better understanding of the significance of this part of the ceremony, he was glad that he had done so.

But it is of considerable interest that Anselm, one of the most learned men of his day, was so ill-informed about the rules which gave Church and state separate roles in the making of a bishop, and which kept the secular authority of the king strictly out of the sacramental part. He was able to get a better understanding of the issues during his own time as Archbishop of Canterbury, because this was the period of the Investiture Contest.

The tale of the Fisher King

The belief in the divine authority of kings is vividly reflected in the tale of the Fisher King, in the Arthurian legends. In the story, the Fisher King (who was sometimes understood to be Joseph of Arimathea), was sick. He could be cured only with the aid of the Holy Grail, the chalice used at the Last Supper, and also the legendary vessel used to catch the blood and water which flowed from the side of Christ when he was on the cross and was 'pierced' by the lances of soldiers (John 19:34). The story mainly concerns the search for this Holy Grail. But it also describes how the whole kingdom was sick because of the sickness of the king. The crops were failing and the cattle were dying. In a way, the Fisher King *was* his country.

The Knights of the Round Table and the Holy Grail from the Legend of King Arthur. French school (15th century).

Church versus state

Troubled by the encroachment of the secular powers upon
the areas where he felt the Church's authority should be
supreme, Pope Gregory VII (1073–85) began to make a bid to
gain the upper hand in the Church–state relationship. The
pope had one supreme weapon for bringing royal personages
to heel, and that was excommunication. An excommunicated
monarch was cut off from all the sacraments, and this was
believed to mean that not only would he himself go to hell
if he died while he was under this 'ban', but so would all his
subjects. (This was on the principle which shapes the 'Fisher
King' legend that a king *is* his kingdom and people, and that
they sink or swim with him.)

The pope did not hesitate to use this method of bringing
the emperor to submit, and the emperor had only his armies
with which to respond. This passage culminated in a meeting
between the pope and the emperor at Canossa, North Italy,
in 1077. Here, the pope made the emperor wait for three
days in the snow and then kiss his stirrup, as a vassal would
a feudal lord, in order to have his excommunication lifted.
The humiliation of the secular authority was not so great as
this made it seem; there were sophisticated politics behind,
and the emperor was able to use the situation to strengthen
his position at home.

But one result was a determination to clarify not only
the particular question of who could make a bishop, and
which parts of the process belonged to the Church and
to the state respectively, but also the wider issue of the
relationship between Church and state. The Concordat of
Worms of 1122 made a distinction between 'temporalities'
and 'spiritualities'. The Church was to have authority over
the 'spiritualities', and the state over the 'temporalities'.
But the two 'arenas' were not so easily separated in real life,
and for the ordinary Christian a bishop was still to be seen
simultaneously as a great lord in the king's retinue and as a
high figure in the Church.

So, one question had not been settled by the device
of trying to separate the spheres of jurisdiction of Church

and state. That was the important question of which was the superior power in the world. Pope Gelasius I (492–96) had used the image of the two swords (Luke 22:49–50) as a convenient way of posing the problem. When Jesus was arrested just before his crucifixion, the disciples produced two swords to try to defend him. In the Vulgate version, Jesus said, 'It is enough' (*satis est*). This was taken literally, as though he had *approved* of the idea that there are two sources of authority in the world. The image was used again in this way by Bernard of Clairvaux, in the book *On Consideration*, which he wrote for Pope Eugenius III. It appears again in Dante's *Monarchia*. The immediacy of the sword as an image of power is characteristically medieval.

CHAPTER 7

The Rebels

The Church spoke of itself from an early period as 'one, holy, catholic and apostolic' Church – that is, a unified Church with the Holy Spirit working in it, which was universal, and which continued in the tradition of Jesus' apostles and, therefore, of Jesus himself. Yet the claim with which this book began, that faith in the Christian world became one seamless robe, with almost the whole population becoming baptized and believing Christians, has to be modified to accommodate the various groups who, over the centuries, either declared themselves separate from the Church or were regarded by the Church as having cut themselves off from it.

In the period of the early Church, it would have been hard to say who were the 'rebels', because no one had yet defined orthodoxy. At first, all Christians were engaged in a common endeavour to establish a shared faith. Hints of early squabbles are to be found in the Acts of the Apostles (for example, Acts 15).

Heresy
The first main division, though it is a complex one, is between 'heretics' and 'schismatics'. The 'heretic' was out of step with the Church on a matter of faith; the schismatic made a 'Church-dividing issue' out of a point of disagreement. The heretic was not the same as the person with doubts. He adopted a belief which questioned, or was at variance with, the Church's official faith, and persisted in it when it was pointed out to him that he could not believe what he did and remain at one in faith with other Christians. The persistence was what made him a heretic. This was not an easy point to arrive at in the first Christian centuries, when much of the faith was still

unmapped, and the Church might have to give time and debate to deciding whether the questioner was right or wrong. The topic of the divine and human natures of Christ, for example, caused immense confusion when questioners began to press for a really clear picture of what was involved.

A leading heretic, or 'heresiarch', could be dangerous in another way. He could become extremely noisy in his insistence that he was right. The 'Arian controversy', so called because it was begun by Arius, caused divisions across Europe during the latter years of the Roman empire. Arians did not accept the divinity of Christ and his full equality as the Son of God with the other persons of the Trinity. Some of the barbarian invaders were 'politically' Arian, as well as Arian in their beliefs.

Schism

A schism was a division of the Church. Schismatics did not, as a rule, set out to create division. They believed themselves to be the true Church. In their view, it was usually others who had gone astray, and when they stood firm against the existing community on a 'Church-dividing issue', schism resulted, with each thereafter holding itself out to be the Church. Schism was taken very seriously in the early Church, because the unity of the Church was itself an article of faith. That, in Augustine's view, made schism a heresy in itself; indeed, he considered it the worst heresy.

Such divisions arose in various ways in the Middle Ages. In Augustine's own lifetime, the followers of Donatus (the 'Donatists') of north Africa were the most pressing example. Between them and the Catholics there was a mutual conviction that the other had gone fundamentally astray. Each believed that it alone had the true succession of ministry in the Church. During times of persecution of Christians, priests and bishops were forced to apostatize, that is, to renounce their faith, and to hand over their Bibles. That made them *traditores*, 'handers-over', the original 'traitors'. Apostasy had always been a serious sin. Many thought it was the sin against the Holy Spirit which Jesus said was the one sin which could not be forgiven (Luke 12:10). Few in the early Church thought a person who had renounced his faith could ever serve again as a priest or bishop. This could present problems about ensuring the succession, because it also meant that a once-apostate bishop could not ordain priests. Augustine wrote many books and letters about the Donatists, who were

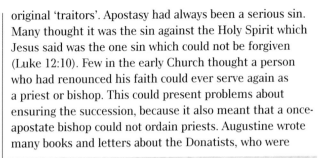

Pope Leo IX excommunicating the Patriarch of Constantinople, beginning the Schism of 1054. Mutual anathemas were exchanged. From a 15th-century Greek manuscript, *The Oracle of Leo the Wise*.

Schism between East and West

The most notable medieval schism was that of 1054. The Greek East and the Latin West had long been estranged by a language division, which made it difficult for them to talk to one another with real mutual understanding. There were resentments about the claim of the Bishop of Rome to be the primate of the whole Church because he was the successor of Peter, the 'rock' on whom Jesus had founded his Church. (Matthew 16:18). In the East, there were other primates – the patriarchs of Jerusalem, Antioch, Alexandria and the imperial city, Constantinople – who took the view that their primacy was not subordinate to that of Rome. Moreover, the Greeks complained, the Christians of the West had departed from the early tradition by making an addition to the Nicene Creed. This was the *filioque* clause, which said that the Holy Spirit proceeded from both the Father and the Son.

It had been added in the West during the eighth century, for clarification, not because the Western Christians wished to alter what they believed had always been the faith of the Church. The Schism between East and West has proved a stubborn one. It was still a source of live resentments in the East during a visit by the pope in 2001, when he tried to make apologies on behalf of the West.

creating difficulties because of an episode of this kind. They refused to accept the legitimacy of a bishop of Carthage, consecrated in 311, because his consecrator had been a *traditor*. The Donatists were, however, orthodox in their faith, if not on this point of 'order' in the Church.

The dualists

There was a third major category of 'unbelievers' visible alongside the Christians in almost every century, and these were the dualists. The earliest 'dualists' were the Gnostics, who existed before the time of Christ. Later came the Manichees, whom Augustine followed for nine or ten years, and then the Albigensians, Cathars and Bogomils of medieval Europe, who clustered in the strip of territory from northern Italy to southern France and northern Spain. They all had certain beliefs in common: there are two 'first principles', or divine originals, in the universe; the God of the Christians is not omnipotent, but is opposed by an evil god, who is his equal in power; matter is evil and is the creation of the evil god. The attraction of all this was that it 'explained' the problem of evil. This was a real difficulty for Christians, for a wholly good God cannot be the author of evil, and if he is omnipotent, why does he allow it? (The solution, devised by Augustine after he had left the Manichee sect in disillusionment, was to say that evil is 'nothing', an 'absence' of good, and that it gets its apparent power from the distance it sets between a person and God.) A feature of the dualist sects was their emphasis on the distinction between a body of the 'elect', who were specially favoured, and the rest of the sect, whose members were merely 'followers'.

Medieval anti-establishment dissidents

A phenomenon which was persistent in the medieval West from the late 12th century was a challenge not to faith, but to order. Popular demagogues, such as Peter of Bruys and Henry of Lausanne, made the leaders of the Church

Opposite page:
Jan Hus being
burned at
the stake.
Illustration from
the *Chronicles
of Ulrich de
Richental*.

John Wyclif
of Oxford
(c. 1320–84), who
became the
founder of the
Lollard movement.
Engraving
by Adolph van
der Laan.

nervous because they were like the charismatic figures of old. They were often calling for things which were orthodox enough in themselves, such as a return to New Testament standards, but they were not always doing it through the proper channels. They were out of control, and so they were seen as a threat.

In the 1170s, the wealthy merchant Waldes, or Valdez, of Lyons had a moment of vision or insight, which led him to think that a movement of renewal was needed in the Church. He and his supporters seem to have intended simply to call the Church back its roots, and to remind it of the example set by Christ and the apostles, the true 'apostolic ministry'.

The Church did not take kindly to this criticism. The Waldensians were excommunicated by the pope at the Council of Verona in 1184, and his movement became one of radical protest. The Waldesians went about in woollen habits, trying to show in their own persons and behaviour the example which they said the clergy should be setting. Waldes made every effort to ensure that it was not he, but Christ, whom his followers regarded as their leader.

The patterns of dissidence which can be seen in the Waldensians reappeared in other forms: in England, in the 14th and early 15th centuries; in the Lollard movement; and in Bohemia, in the Hussite movement.

John Wyclif was an Oxford master who argued from an academic point of view about a number of issues: the imbalance of power he perceived in the Church; the growth of monarchical pretensions on the part of the papacy; the unacceptability of some Christians thinking that they were 'better' than others (he meant the monks and friars, in particular); and the need to get back to scripture as the touchstone of Christian teaching. These ideas struck a chord with popular discontent and groups of ordinary Christians began to put about these so-called 'Lollard' ideas. Some of them met in house groups

Jan Hus

Jan Hus was born in the early 1370s in Bohemia. He was ordained priest in 1400, and taught at the University of Prague in the first decade of the 15th century.

In 1403, a list of already condemned 'Articles of John Wyclif' was sent to the office of the archbishop by a disturbed German master, together with 21 'articles' Hus had added. On request, Hus duly delivered up his own copies. He soon found himself under accusation as a Wycliffite heretic. The more vigorously and publicly he defended himself and his orthodoxy, the more insistent became the accusations.

Hus was now caught in the familiar trap of medieval 'heretics', from which he could escape neither by 'proving his innocence' nor by 'recantation'. As he attempted to 'explain himself', he was gradually drawn into clearer and clearer statements of positions which began to look very like Wycliffite heresies. He said that God ordered the preaching of his word throughout the world. He said that if the pope were to forbid this, then he was a false witness, and that this was a disobedience to God's will which ought to be punished.

In 1411, Hus was excommunicated by the pope. At the Council of Constance in 1415, Hus was brought to trial. He went there under a promised safe-conduct, but he soon found that again he was naïve in expecting that he would be given a fair hearing, or a hearing at all (there was an attempt to try him in his absence).

By this stage, the Czech nobility was now involved, and the battle over Hus had become tangled up with high politics and the power struggle between Church and state. Hus was condemned, and died at the stake in 1415. A martyr can be extremely influential after his death, and Hus became a national hero. His writings, especially those of the later period – when he had been thinking out, under challenge and threat, a body of now quite radical teaching on the nature of the Church – gained a lasting influence, notably on Luther.

and studied the Bible in English. The conviction began to grow that laypeople could find their own way to a true faith simply by reading the Bible for themselves.

In reaction to this worrying trend, apologists wrote defences of the Church. Reginald Pecock's *The Repressor of Over Much Blaming of the Clergy*, written in about 1449, accepted that the clergy had some faults, but Pecock did not think that they were as bad as they were painted. He identified 'three opinions' as 'the cause and ground of many of the errors which many of the lay party hold, and by which holding they unjustly and overmuch blame the clergy'. The first mistaken opinion was that there was no legitimate government, except what was laid down in scripture. The second was that each individual Christian, reading scripture for himself, 'shall without fail and default find the true understanding of Scripture'. This notion rested on the confidence that the Holy Spirit would lead the reader safely to the right conclusions. It cut out the Church's teaching role and took away its control of what people believed, so it was an idea much frowned upon in the Church. This was coupled with the third dangerous opinion, which was that the individual who had read his Bible need not respect what the Church taught.

Dissidents as dangerous

It is not hard to see why such attitudes were seen as dangerous, not only by the official Church, but also by the state. Among the political poems and satires which survive from the 14th century is one about the Council of London in 1382, which describes the whole kingdom as disturbed, because it is not spiritually 'right'. There are earthquakes and uprisings of the peasants; the 'ship of state' is foundering. The world is turned upside down.

In another poem, we read that the Church is God's garden, but that Satan fills it with weeds because he is God's enemy. These weeds are the Lollards. 'There has been no worse pestilence in the Church,' the poem

'I am accused by my adversaries before your Paternity's Grace as if I were a scandalous and erroneous preacher, contrary to the Holy Mother Church, and thus wandering from the faith. With God's help, I wish to refute the scandalous accusations of my enemies.'

JAN HUS
(c. 1369–1415),
LETTERS

continues. The traditional cry of a Church frightened by the sheer success of dissident movements is also in this poem: 'The simple are being led astray... The poison is getting everywhere.' But there is a new complaint in the poem, that heresies and schisms of the past have been guilty of a single error. These Lollards are full of errors; they challenge everything.

Returned to the fold by force?

It was accepted from the first centuries that if someone who had been a heretic or schismatic wanted to return to the Church, he or she could do so, provided that there had been a valid baptism. This meant baptism with water, in the name of the Father, Son and Holy Spirit. Baptism could, in an emergency, be carried out by someone who was not ordained, so there was no difficulty about the ministry. Valid baptism could be carried out in a schismatic or heretical sect. Baptism could not be repeated, so there was to be no question of 'rebaptizing' the convert. All that was looked for was repentance and the return to the fold, and then, in Augustine's view, the 'valid' baptism became 'efficacious', and the person's sins were forgiven.

'Nobility is in servitude and the peasantry rules.'

ANONYMOUS,
14TH CENTURY

The responses of the medieval Church were more vigorous. The scene was different. Now the monolith of the unified Church in the West was sufficiently integrated to make it possible for the Church to act decisively. It did so in two main ways. The first took the form of a 'crusade' against the dualist groups called the Albigensians, in the south of France and northern Spain, in an attempt to convert by force. The second had an element of force, too. The 'Inquisition' was profoundly repressive. It used excommunication, confiscation of property and banishment to frighten people into 'returning' to the fold. It would even brand people who resisted. From 1157, perpetual imprisonment was a possibility.

Beginning in the 1230s in Langedoc and Lombardy, an inquisition was set up from time to time to 'examine' suspected heretics, a machinery created by Pope Gregory IX. Bishops were required to appoint people in each parish to inform the authorities about the local heretics. These were to be the witnesses to synods. Members of the mendicant orders of monks were 'used' by the papacy to help to 'run' the Inquisition system. Neighbours were encouraged to inform on one another. Terrified peasants were called upon to explain their views on complex theological questions.

The 'questions' used to test for heresy became quite standard. In a surviving text on Lollard inquiries, the

The punishment by burning of those the Inquisition found guilty of heresy or witchcraft.

Fasciculi zizaniorum ('Bundles of Weeds'), the repetition of certain points is striking. The reality may be that the witch-hunting of the heretics was creating a body of 'wrong opinion' by remorselessly putting it into the mouths of bewildered and uneducated people. It is not impossible that our picture of what heretics really believed is distorted in this way, for there is, in general, far more to read in the Middle Ages from the 'official' Church's side than from the side of the heretics and dissidents themselves.

There was an apparent pastoral intention in all this, for those who recanted would get a light penalty, such as wearing a yellow cross and going on a pilgrimage, and could be considered to have been 'saved'. But just as in the present day police forces may be encouraged to make arrests so as to increase their numbers of 'cases solved', so in this medieval policing of orthodoxy in the faith it is to be expected that offences were being artificially 'created'. A peasant who was unsure about what he was being accused of would be wise to 'recant', just to be on the safe side. There were distinctions here, however, because a good test of a real Waldensian or Lollard might be that he understood very well what he believed, and would not swear falsely or recant before the tribunal of the Inquisition.

It is not surprising that this kind of conduct on the part of the authorities led to a sense of persecution among the Waldensians and Lollards. Lollard literature is particularly eloquent on this subject.

Is there salvation outside the Church?
The presumption on which the Inquisition – and, indeed, all dealing with dissidence, heresy and schism in the medieval centuries in the West – rested was that there was no salvation outside the Church (*nulla salus extra ecclesiam*). 'Interfaith dialogue' was not a possibility, unless it had the objective of converting the unbelievers to orthodox Christian faith, and those outside the Church, because they were Jews or Muslims, were deemed lost souls.

Another way of seeming to be 'outside the Church' was to engage in the kind of uncontrollable 'charismatic' preaching or writing which caused the early Church so much anxiety, because there seemed no way to ensure that such 'prophetic', and often extremely attractive, figures would not lead the faithful astray. One example from the East at the beginning of our period was Maximus the Confessor. He was born in about 580, and moved from a

'They dismissed
the holy old
man into
prison... [His
disciples were
left] naked and
hungry, having
only God's help.'

ANONYMOUS,
SEVENTH CENTURY

'The divine plan
I seem to
understand in
the scriptures,
especially since
some monks
have most
urgently
advised me,
that I have an
obligation not
to keep silent
about the wrath
of the Judge so
soon to be
revealed from
heaven upon all
the wickedness
and injustice of
men who are
unwilling to do
penance for
their sins.'

JOACHIM OF FIORE
(c. 1132–1202)

career in public life to become a monk. He eventually became a respected figure, partly for his writing about the importance of the correct formulation of the doctrine of the person of Christ. But he was put on trial, and his disciples were sent into exile.

Another example was Joachim, the Abbot of Fiore, who, at the end of the 12th century, seems to have begun the later medieval fashion for describing the pope as Antichrist. The rabble-rousing flavour of his writing made him disturbing to ecclesiastical officialdom.

Who decides what is the true faith?

The phenomenon of the honest dissident raises an important question about the way in which it was 'decided' who was right. The Middle Ages recognized the same two ways for the Church to reach a decision as the early Church. One was by official pronouncements by a council or a pope, the other by the emerging of the *consensus fidelium*, or 'consent of the whole people of God'. In practice, these had been complementary. There have been striking examples of the Church officially ruling that something was unacceptable which, a few centuries, later quietly became accepted.

Attempts at conversion

There are instances of serious attempts at conversion. In the mid-12th century, Peter the Venerable, the Abbot of Cluny, arranged for a translation of the Qur'an into Latin to be made, so that Christians talking to Muslims could have a better sense of the differences of belief involved. In the same period, several dialogues between Jews and Christians were published, again so as to clarify the difference of belief. One autobiographical account of the conversion of a Jew survives, Hermannus Judaeus' *De conversione sua*. Hermannus described how he had resisted for a long time the conclusion to which he was now forced to come, that the Jews had been content with the rough outer husk of scripture, while the Christians had enjoyed its sweet kernel.

Having the Bible in the language of ordinary people is one example. Allowing the laity to receive wine as well as the bread at the eucharist, or holy communion, is another. On the other hand, the *consensus fidelium* needed to be expressed through some 'official' channel, if everyone was to be clear what it was.

At the end of the Middle Ages, this was all becoming somewhat unbalanced by the increasing claims of the

The Council of Trent in 1512 deliberating about the decisions they were making on behalf of the Church.

papacy to plenitude of power. In the mid-15th century, Nicholas of Cusa wrote a *Catholic Concordance*, in which he made various suggestions for the solving of contemporary problems in the Church. Among them was discussion of the ways in which the opinions of the faithful as a whole, or at least of ordinary people, could be included.

Clues in the creeds

By the medieval period, the Nicene Creed of the fourth century was well established and, from the eighth century in the West, the Apostles' Creed was also in use. The clauses in these creeds which reflect the early controversies also helped Christian 'apologists', or defenders of the faith, to 'classify' heresies which reappeared in later centuries. The claim that heretics were preaching 'novelties' was very common, and yet the 'novelties' were also usually identified with the 'novelties' of other, earlier heretics.

Clauses in the creeds were used to argue against views which were considered heretical by the organized Church.

'I think that qualified learned laymen should be included in making decisions since the common good of the Church is being sought.'

NICHOLAS OF CUSA,
*THE CATHOLIC
CONCORDANCE*, 1433

Dualism

Dualists, such as the Gnostics, Manichees, Cathars, Bogomils and Albigensians, believed that there were two opposed forces, or gods, in the universe, engaged in eternal warfare. They believed that matter was the work of the evil god. Clauses in the Nicene Creed (N) and the Apostles' Creed (A) counter this view:

I believe in God the Father Almighty, Maker of heaven and earth. (A)

I believe in one God the Father Almighty (N)
Maker of heaven and earth (N)
And of all things visible and invisible. (N)

These clauses emphasize that there is only one God and that he is omnipotent and the maker of the physical world.

Christology

Some groups, such as the Arians, doubted the divinity and humanity of Christ. These clauses in the creeds emphasize Christ's divinity:

And in Jesus Christ his only Son our Lord (A)
Who was conceived by the Holy Ghost (A)

And in one Lord Jesus Christ, the only-begotten Son of God (N)
Begotten of his Father before all worlds (N)
God of God, light of light (N)
Very God of very God (N)
Begotten not made (N)
Being of one substance with the Father (N)
By whom all things were made (N)

The following clauses stress Christ's humanity:

Born of the Virgin Mary (A)

Who for us men and for our salvation came down from
   heaven (N)
And was incarnate by the Holy Ghost of the Virgin Mary (N)
And was made man. (N)

Some heretics over the centuries questioned the resurrection, which was of central importance to the Christian faith. Everything turned on this, because it showed the power of God in Christ, and gave assurance to the faithful that they were saved and could hope for heaven. Only if Jesus was really the Son of God, and was really human, and really died and was resurrected was the Christian faith not in vain. The following clauses emphasize these points:

Suffered under Pontius Pilate (A)
Was crucified, dead, and buried. (A)
He descended into hell (A)

'How false it is when many learned theologians speak disparagingly about us Wittenberg theologians, alleging that we are disseminating novelties. They speak as though there would not have been people in the past and in other places who said what we say.'

MARTIN LUTHER
(1483–1546)

The third day he rose again from the dead (A)
He ascended into heaven (A)

And was crucified also for us under Pontius Pilate (N)
He suffered and was buried, and the third day he rose again
  according to the Scriptures (N)
And ascended into heaven (N)

Questioning whether Christ was really to be the judge of mankind was also an aspect of this area of asking awkward 'heretical' questions which went to the heart of the faith. This point, too, is made quite clear in the creeds:

And sitteth on the right hand of God the Father Almighty (A)
From thence he shall come to judge the quick and the
  dead (A)

An 11th-century dome mosaic in Florence, showing the fate of those condemned to hell at the Last Judgment. *The Damned of the Last Judgment.*

And sitteth on the right hand of the Father (N)
And he shall come again with glory to judge both the quick
*   and the dead (N)*
Whose Kingdom shall have no end (N)

Trinity

Questions about the Holy Spirit turned on his divinity, and
on his equality with the Father and the Son. The area of
dispute here tended to be whether the Holy Spirit was
truly divine and not merely some sort of animating force
in the world (the 'world soul'), as some 'late Platonists'
had said. The creeds clarified this issue:

I believe in the Holy Ghost (A)

And I believe in the Holy Ghost (N)
The Lord and giver of life (N)

Who proceedeth from the Father and the Son (N)
Who with the Father and the Son together is worshipped and
   glorified (N)
Who spake by the prophets (N)

The full explication of the doctrine of the Trinity in the
West came with Augustine, who stressed, above all, the
equality and co-eternity of the three persons of the
Godhead.

The Church
Questions about the role and nature and authority of the
Church became much more complex in the West in the
Middle Ages. At the time of the formulation of the creeds,
the main thing which needed to be stressed was the fact
that the Church was one – it was a single 'communion',
or *koinonia*, a particular kind of community, which could
also be thought of as the 'body', whose 'head' is Christ. It
was 'universal', or 'catholic' (one Church throughout the
world). It was 'apostolic', which meant that it was engaged
in mission, as Jesus had said he meant it to be, and in
continuity with his teaching. It was 'holy'. The creeds
made clear these points:

The holy Catholic church. (A)
The Communion of Saints (A) [Note that 'saints' simply
means those who are holy, that is, the faithful.]

And I believe in one catholic and apostolic Church (N)

Human destiny
Questions about sin and the forgiveness of sin, and the
role of the sacraments, arose in much more complicated
ways in the Middle Ages. However, at the time of the
formation of the creeds, one key question was whether
the Church had the authority to declare God's forgiveness
of sins. The creeds set out the Church's understanding
about these issues:

The forgiveness of sins (A)

I acknowledge one baptism for the remission of sins (N)

Questions about the purpose and end of human life were still in the early stages of consideration when the creeds were completed. However, there is an indication of the continuing importance of the battle to outlaw dualism, in that it had to be stressed that not only the soul, but also the material body, would be resurrected:

The resurrection of the body (A)
and the life everlasting (A)

And I look for the resurrection of the dead, and the life of the
    world to come (N)

CHAPTER   8

Monks, Saints and Christian Examples

'Have no other
occupation or
meditation than
the cry of "Lord
Jesus Christ,
Son of God,
have mercy on
me." Under no
circumstances
give yourself
any rest. This
practice
prevents your
spirit from
wandering and
makes it
impregnable
and inaccessible
to the
suggestions of
the enemy.'

NICEPHORUS,
ITALIAN HESYCHAST
ON MOUNT ATHOS,
14TH CENTURY

Time to spend thinking at leisure about philosophical matters in conversation with friends was highly prized in the ancient world. It was fashionable for figures in public life to express a wistfulness for such *otium*, or intellectual leisure. Sometimes, like Cicero, they acted this out and did, indeed, spend time in retirement writing on such themes as duty, friendship and old age. Augustine of Hippo had had the same wish as a young man, and when he became a Christian in 386, he left his professorship as a teacher of oratory, and acted on it. He retreated with a group of friends, his son and his mother, to Cassiciacum on Lake Como, to discuss and then to write about *The Happy Life*, *Order* and other such subjects, in which both classical philosophy and Christianity shared an interest. When he went back to north Africa, he set up a community in which he and his friends could lead a monastic life, apart from the world, studying scripture and praying. Augustine's contemporary, Jerome, the translator of the Vulgate version of the Bible, felt the same tug, and he, too, made a series of attempts to live apart from the world.

In both East and West, the 'call' to the Christian version of this life of 'philosophical retirement' had a focus with an important difference from the old 'philosopher's version'. 'Reading' and 'thinking' remained central to the religious life in the West. Communities of individuals, and individuals on their own, chose from the earliest Christian centuries to set themselves apart from the world in this way.

The Jesus prayer

In the East, the emphasis was more strongly upon an affective and transcendental spirituality. Gregory Palamas, who wrote between 1338 and 1341, was approved by the Synod of Constantinople of 1368 as a Father and a Doctor of the Church. By this time, there was a strong hermit tradition in the East, known as 'Hesychasm'. Gregory helped to bring into focus and to defend the essential activity of the Orthodox monk-hermit. Such a believer was trying to achieve a permanent state of mental prayer. The prayer which was used was known as the 'Jesus prayer', and the hermit said the name of Jesus in his mind, day and night, throughout his life, putting into practice Psalm 34:8, 'Taste and see that the Lord is good' (Authorized Version).

Gregory Palamas was a monk himself, from the age of 20, in the Great Lavra on Mount Athos. He had to leave in 1341 because of the threat posed by Turkish raids on the Mount Athos peninsula. He sought refuge in Thessalonika in northern Greece, where he lived in a spiritual circle of

A monastery on Mount Athos, Greece, in which the living areas enclose the great church.

friends, practising the Jesus prayer. From 1325 to 1326, he
was an abbot, at the monastery of Esphigmenou.

Dispute and debate

Gregory then became involved in a dispute with Barlaam,
who was rebuked by two Councils of Constantinople.
Barlaam thought that monks were intellectually inferior,
and that the practices of those who put the emphasis on
spirituality were less impressive and less important than
those of philosopher-theologians. Barlaam also accused
the Hesychasts of many of the same offences as those
with which the Lollards were charged in the West. He said
that they rejected the need for social responsibility, they
did not put a proper weight on the importance of the
sacraments and they had charismatic tendencies.

Barlaam's debate with Gregory led to Gregory writing
the *Triads*. They were arguing about the question of the
extent to which purely spiritual effort and activity can bring
a person to God, and whether the body as well as the mind
can be transfigured by the divine illumination which is shed
upon the devout and prayerful soul. Is this a way in which
someone can truly 'know God', even if he does not have the
intellectual understanding of a trained theologian? Many
monks in the East had invested their lives in the trust
that this was possible; indeed, for them, it was the best
way to do it. Gregory explored the idea of *theosis*, the
'deification' by which man, 'made in God's image and
likeness' (Genesis 1:26), returned to a communion with
God in which he became truly 'like God'.

Baarlam had accused the Hesychasts of something
close to dualism, and of being 'Messalians', because they
were 'pretending' to contemplate the essence of God with
their bodily eyes. Gregory discussed this in the *Triads*, too,
explaining carefully the attitude of these monks to the
body – always a difficult question for medieval Christianity,
because it was so suspicious of the body as a vessel of
temptation.

For professed religious people, such as monks, nuns and

*'As for us, we
think the mind
becomes evil
through
dwelling on
fleshly thoughts,
but that there is
nothing bad in
the body, since
the body is not
evil in itself.'*

GREGORY PALAMAS
(c. 1296–1359)

hermits, in both East and West, the crucial thing was the call to a way of life which would make it possible to 'go apart' and spend time with God in prayer and worship. Prayer was the *opus dei*, the 'work of God'.

The ascetic life

To try to become a monk, nun or hermit was to attempt to obey to the full the commandment to love God with all one's heart. It was also, especially in the Middle Ages, understood to be a fulfilment of the command to love one's neighbour, for the monk or nun was also praying for the world and for other people. It was even considered to be the special task of members of religious orders to perform this task for the world. There were those who prayed, those who ruled (ran things) and those who did the work, said Adalbero in the 11th century, and the most important of these to society were those who prayed.

Nevertheless, there were fundamental differences in the structure and pattern of the lives of those who committed themselves to God in this special way in both the East and the West. In the East, the Desert Fathers set the pattern. They were hermits who adopted various extreme forms of life, and came to be regarded as powerhouses of spiritual influence and as authorities who could assist ordinary people with their problems. The Stylites, for example, lived on platforms on high poles, and were an object of reverence to those who came to ask their spiritual advice. Others, shut off from the world in caves or huts, sought to deny themselves any contact with the temptations of 'the world', especially with women. This was an aspect of the contemporary preoccupation with the dangers of the flesh, which was partly a legacy of the dualists' conviction that matter was evil and that only spirit was good.

In the East, there continued to be a preference for idiorrhythmic living, that is, a free choice by the religious as to the way he would plan his day. Monks lived largely in their cells, and met only at intervals to eat and pray

'Man has been created to praise, reverence and serve God our Lord, and by this means to save his soul; and the other things upon the face of the earth are created for man, and to help him in the prosecution of the end for which he is created.'

IGNATIUS LOYOLA
(1491/5–1556)

together. Many of the early religious of the East were hermits, living entirely alone. Indeed, such figures can still be seen on Mount Athos, the holy mountain in northern Greece, living lives of solitude and prayer in cells high on the cliffs, on food lowered to them in baskets.

The crucial development in the West took place when, in the sixth century, Benedict of Nursia (c. 480–550) withdrew with a group of friends to try to live an ascetic life. This prompted him to give serious thought to the way in which the 'religious life' should be organized.

Benedict arranged, at first, for groups of 12 monks to live together in small communities. Then he moved to Montecassino where, in about 529, he set up the monastery which was to become the mother house of the Benedictine Order. The rule of life he drew up was a synthesis of

A late-medieval impression of St Benedict giving his Rule to the monks of his order. The kneeling monks have their hair cut in the 'tonsure'. By Turino di Vanni.

elements in existing 'rules', particularly the 'Rule of the Master' (whose origins are uncertain). From this point onwards in the West, the Rule of St Benedict set the standard pattern for living the religious life until the 12th century.

In the Anglo-Saxon period in England, nuns were already forming a significant proportion of the part of the population drawn to the religious life, and there were several

The Rule of St Benedict

The Rule of St Benedict achieved a good working balance. It aimed at moderation and orderliness. Those who went apart from the world to live lives dedicated to God should not, he felt, subject themselves to extreme asceticism. They should live in poverty and chastity, and in obedience to their abbot, but they should not feel the need routinely to 'subjugate the flesh'

with scourges and hair-shirts. They should eat moderately, but they should not starve themselves to the point of death. They should divide their time in a regular and orderly way between manual work, reading and prayer – the *opus dei*, or 'work of God', which was the chief activity and purpose of their lives. There were to be seven regular acts of worship in the day, known as 'hours', attended by the whole community. In Benedict's vision the yoke was to be sweet and the burden light. The monastery was a 'school' of the Lord's service, in which the baptized soul made progress in the Christian life.

'double monasteries', where communities of monks and communities of nuns lived side by side. Certain abbesses proved to be outstanding figures in a way which was then difficult for women to achieve in their own right. Hilda, Abbess of Whitby (614–80) was of royal birth, in the kingdom of Northumbria. Her sister became a nun, and Hilda wanted to follow her. However, Aidan, one of the principal figures among the Christians of the Celtic tradition, made her the abbess of a religious house in the north of England. In 659, she founded a 'double monastery' at Whitby, where she was able to exert an influence on Aidan's side at the Synod of Whitby in 664, when the Celtic and Roman Christians had a conference to try to sort out their differences.

Nobility and patronage in the religious life

Another common feature of monastic life in the West was also already evident, in Hilda's story. It was largely reserved for the upper classes. The serfs did not have the freedom to choose to become monks. The houses of monks and nuns became the recipients of noble and royal patronage. 'Spare' children of good birth would be given to the religious life by their families as 'child oblates', and would then be in a position to discharge on behalf of the family the role of 'pray-er' for the souls of their relations. Similarly, rich and powerful families would give monasteries lands and estates, for the good of the souls of their members. Rulers and soldiers were too busy to attend to their spiritual lives as they should, and 'professionals' drawn from their own families could help them by doing it on their behalf.

One consequence of this was that, in the later Middle Ages in particular, the abbot or abbess was usually a nobleman or woman. She was often chosen because of being the highest in birth in the monastery or convent, and not because of any natural powers of leadership or outstanding spirituality. Chaucer's cruel 14th-century caricature of a prioress depicts a woman who would have been much more at home in a country house playing with her lapdogs:

There was also a nun, a prioress
   That of her smiling was full simple and coy…
Of small hounds had she, that she fed
   With roasted flesh, or milk and stale bread…
Full seemly her wimple pinched was.

CHAUCER, *CANTERBURY TALES*, PROLOGUE (1387–88)

In these features of noble patronage of the religious life lay not only the stamp of society's approval, but also the potential for decay. Houses which became very rich, and which were filled with individuals who had not chosen to enter the religious life, but had been put into it in childhood, could also become decadent. The so-called Cluniac reforms of the 10th century were a consequence of the recognition that, from time to time, there would need to be a tightening up if the Benedictine religion was not to be lost sight of. At Cluny and the houses which imitated it, standards were high, although here, too, there was a danger of distortion of the original Benedictine vision. Cluniac houses had extra rules and a degree of rigidity which compromised the original simplicity of the Benedictine life.

The Prioress from Chaucer's *The Canterbury Tales*. From the 'Ellesmere' Chaucer (1400–10).

Experimentation

At the end of the 11th century, several developments radically altered the range of choice for those in the West who wanted to enter the religious life. The first was a change of fashion, which encouraged married couples of mature years to decide to end their days in monastic life. A knight who had fought his wars might make an agreement with his wife that they would go off into separate religious houses. Adult entry of this sort was entry by people who really did want to be monks and nuns, and it had the potential to alter the balance in favour of serious commitment. We saw in chapter 1 Guibert of Nogent's comment on this issue, in his autobiography. The new emphasis was on a return to the concept of personal 'vocation' to the religious life, which made people see it as the 'divine call' it used to be in the first Christian centuries.

These mature adults were not the only category of the new 'volunteer religious'. Younger people were being drawn in, too. At Bec, earlier in the 11th century, Herluin, himself an ex-soldier, had founded a new religious house. Lanfranc, a famous teacher, joined him there, and set up a school to which the sons of the local people were invited to come. They flocked there, according to the historian Orderic Vitalis, and some of them stayed. When Anselm, Lanfranc's successor, ran the school, it was for the actual young monks of Bec.

The Cistercians

Out of the period of experiment came one immensely important new order, the Cistercians. They used the Benedictine rule, but they had a different set of priorities. The first was a determination to protect themselves from the dangers which could come from growing too rich. They chose to build houses in remote places. They made a place for people from the lower social classes who had vocations. These were to be lay brothers.

The startling early success of this order was due to Bernard of Clairvaux. When he decided to enter the newly founded house of Cîteaux, he took with him a group of his relations and friends. He set a fashion, and so rapidly did recruitment proceed that more and more houses had to be founded in quick succession. He himself was made abbot of one of them, Clairvaux, at so early an age that, at first, the responsibility made him ill. But he went on to become a leading figure in the monastic world, and in the world of politics. He spoke so well and so movingly that he was useful as a diplomatic emissary, as well as a preacher.

The same period saw a number of experiments in the religious life, some of them short-lived, or nothing more than the eccentric behaviour of one individual disillusioned with conventional provisions. Henry the Monk is an example of a former monk who became a popular demagogue in the early 12th century. But so many were seriously engaged in pushing forward the boundaries of the religious life that one writer thought it would be helpful to review the available modes of living for the religious in the 12th century. This *De diversis ordinibus* covered all the possibilities, from Benedictines and reformed Benedictines, to the canons – priests who

Ribbed vaulting at the Cistercian abbey of Fontenay shows that the taste for plainness did not stop the Cistercians sometimes building on a large scale.

did not live enclosed lives, but who were allowed to work in the world – and the various sorts of hermits.

The only real rival to the Rule of St Benedict was the 'Rule' of Augustine, which was adopted by 'regular canons'. These differed from monks, in that they were priests who could be active in the community, for example, serving in parishes. They were not living under the monastic rule of 'stability', which, in principle, confined a monk for life to the house in which he was professed. Canons of cathedrals, in particular, were encouraged to live in community under a rule, and the Augustinian rule was well-adapted to their needs.

The 12th century saw the creation of new orders in a similar mould. The Victorines in Paris produced leading academic figures and teachers of 'spirituality', such as Hugh, Andrew and Richard of St Victor. The Premonstratensians were associated with their own leading figures, like Anselm of Havelberg, who made an attempt to sit down with Greek Christians and discuss the differences which were dividing them from the West. Anslem wrote an account of these early 'ecumenical dialogues' in his own *Dialogues*.

The rise of the mendicants

From the beginning of the 13th century there were orders of friars dedicated to preaching. These were the mendicants. The Franciscans were founded by Francis of Assisi, and they concentrated chiefly on preaching to ordinary Christians and trying to bring alive for them the spirit of the apostolic life, as Jesus had taught it to his disciples. The Dominicans were founded by St Dominic, specifically to preach against the heretics in the south of France and elsewhere.

The Franciscans faced a crisis when St Francis died, as many religious movements have done when they were begun by a particularly charismatic individual. The essence of St Francis's way was peculiarly dependent on his personality. On his death, some of his followers were anxious to keep to this extreme life of poverty and

'Since... many kinds of callings have come into being, and particularly in own day, institutions of monks and canons differing in habit and worship are increasing, it is necessary to show, with God's help, how such servants of God differ and what the purposes of the different forms of callings are.'

AUTHOR UNKNOWN,
BOOK ON THE
DIFFERENT ORDERS,
12TH CENTURY

simplicity. Others recognized that the long-term survival of the order would require it to become 'institutionalized'. To the first group were attracted a number of individuals on the 'fringe' of religious respectability. There resulted a great debate about poverty.

Attitudes to the friars became extremely complex. Their sermons seem to have been popular with people starved of an adequate supply of preaching from the parish pulpit. Margery Kempe describes 'how fast the people came running to hear the sermon' when they heard that a famous preacher had come to King's Lynn. But people could also be choosy. Margery Kempe also notes how they would not sit down and compose themselves to listen, but would stand impatiently so that they could easily walk out if they did not like what they heard. Some, she said, came with their sins unrepented and, indeed, with no intention of giving up their bad ways. Some – and this is reported of sermon-goers in other centuries – went only to be seen, for the sermon was a local 'occasion', at which it might be fashionable to be present. Others, she said, were there not to listen to the content, but to sample the style.

St Dominic (c. 1170–1221), who founded the 'Friars Preachers' to preach the true faith to the heretics. By Giovanni Bellini (1515).

On the other hand, because of their mendicant way of life, there was a risk that some friars would fall into corrupt habits. The resentment against the clergy, which mounted in dissident communities in the late-medieval centuries, was prompted most strongly by the sight of wealth and indolence among the higher clergy, but it was also difficult for ordinary people to feel respect for local clergy if they were ignorant and incompetent. Some of that resentment spilled over into criticism of the friars for similar, and other, faults. When these visible shortcomings were coupled with the Church's insistence that heaven was to be reached only 'within the Church' and with the aid of its sacraments, articulate laypeople were naturally resentful.

From the point of view of 'officialdom', the friars were unsettling. On the one hand they represented the Church: they were members of the clergy; the Franciscan and Dominican orders had had papal approval since the beginning of the 13th century, and they were highly educated preachers. Yet, partly perhaps because they wandered the countryside preaching, the friars sometimes

Jibes against the friars

There are jibes which suggested that the friars did, indeed, get a bad name. A 'Song Against the Friars', an anonymous 14th-century verse, put it satirically. There are those who claimed to be learned, who 'give themselves to great study'; and others who:

Men may see by their countenance,
  That they are men of great penance.

But the author had never, in the 40 years of his life, seen fatter men than these friars:

Priest, nor monk, nor yet canon
  Nor any man of religion,
Gives him so to devotion,
  As do these holy friars.
For some give themselves to chivalry,
  Some to riot and ribaldry.

became associated in the eyes of 'authority' with fringe movements, such as the Lollards.

The higher calling

The not-always-edifying story of the reality of living the monastic, or 'religious', life in the Middle Ages should not be allowed to detract too much from the central ideals. There is every reason to suppose that many, living quietly in religious houses, prayed, read and – if they were Benedictines – did hard manual labour, with the utmost devotion, throughout their lifetimes. There were spiritual giants among the mendicants, as well as thoroughly bad examples to their fellow men and women. This idea of setting an example was an important one.

After Augustine of Canterbury brought the faith to England it was said that it was as though the sun had come out. Also among 'God's athletes', Bernard of Clairvaux counts St Malachi, whose *Life* he wrote in the 12th century, emphasizing its value as an example. One of the main attractions for medieval people of the cult of saints was the reassurance that some had managed to lead exemplary lives, and had shown others how to do it.

The requirements for sanctity were relatively easy to stereotype. In the *Life of St Erkenwald*, we read that he was 'perfect in wisdom, modest in conversation, vigilant in prayer, chaste in body, dedicated to holy reading, rooted in charity'. By the late 11th century, it was even possible to hire a hagiographer, such as Osbern of Canterbury, who would come and write a *Life* of a dead abbot, in the hope that he would be canonized. It was usual to include a list of miraculous interventions by the saint, as indications that he or she had had divine approval. Here again, the corrupting effects of real life are evident. There was active competition to achieve canonization, because an abbey with a saint among its former membership could hope for pilgrims to come and visit the 'shrine'. There would also be relics and, with luck, stories of miracles brought about by those relics.

'After the passion and resurrection of the Lord, when the Catholic faith had been diffused throughout the world, there were "God's athletes" sowing the seed of the faith.'

ANONYMOUS, *LIFE OF ST ERKENWALD*

A 'reliquary', or container for the relics of a saint, from the 12th century. This one is made of gold. The richness of such containers shows how precious their contents were.

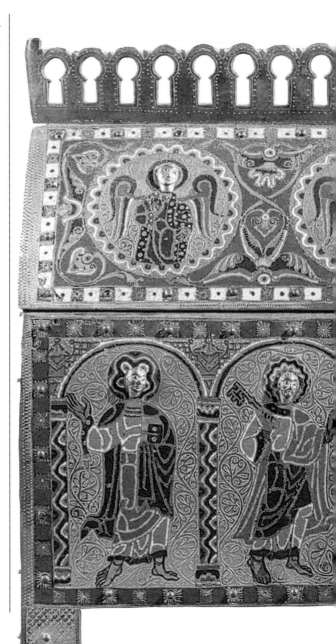

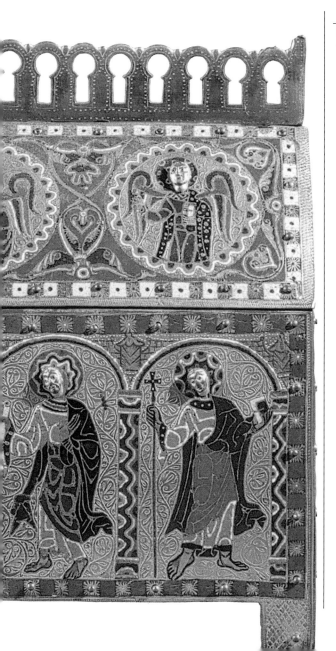

This meant that there is about the phenomenon of the saints, both an inward and an outward aspect. A holy man or woman was thought to leave behind, in objects touched or places visited, a residual power, a 'merit', which pious people could acquire for their assistance in their own troubles by going on pilgrimage and praying at the shrine. A similar power inhered in the body of the saint, or in parts of the body, such as the fingernails or hair, which could conveniently be kept in little 'relic-holders' or reliquaries.

Simple people would use these, praying and touching the holy items, in the hope of miracles of healing – rather as people still visit the comparatively modern shrine at Lourdes or, in the Greek Orthodox world, go to the shrine at Tinos, where the 'saint' is the blessed Virgin, Jesus' mother. This, though mysterious and spiritual power, is outward in the sense that the consciousness of the devout was fixed on the material objects and in the places in which the power was believed to reside.

A better picture of what went on 'inside' a saint or an ordinary member of the religious orders trying to take his or her faith seriously is to be obtained from the comments of those whose writings survive, for here we have more evidence than can be got from stories of their activities and the miraculous consequences. The most frequent comment heard from those later rated 'saints' was the difficulty they had in keeping an appropriate balance between their active and their contemplative lives. We hear this from Gregory the Great, pope in the year 600; from Aldhelm, an abbot of Malmesbury, who was not canonized himself, in the seventh and eighth centuries; and so on until Bernard of Clairvaux wrote a book in five volumes for Pope Eugenius III, called *On Consideration*.

The balance between the active and the contemplative life was, indeed, perhaps the core issue for those who aspired to be spiritual giants and examples to others, or for those who simply wanted to be good Christians (for a true saint is, of course, also humble). How much time should be given to

'Love flies, runs and leaps for joy; it is free and unrestrained. Love gives all for all, resting in one who is highest above all things, from whom every good flows and proceeds.'

THOMAS À KEMPIS,
THE IMITATION OF CHRIST, c. 1418

God and how much to work in the world? Ironically, the idea that some people could be left to carry out the work of prayer for the world as professionals does not seem to have relieved them of this sense of the crowding demands of ordinary life. Anselm of Canterbury begins his *Proslogion* with the advice that the 'little man' (*homunculus*) who wanted to concentrate on God should withdraw into the chamber of his own mind, close the door and shut out the multitude of irrelevant thoughts which would otherwise crowd in upon him and distract him. There, a great liberation was to be found.

Holy War

C hrist brought a message of peace and reconciliation.
People of his time expected him to be a revolutionary,
but he always sought to change things without
violence, except on the occasion when he threw the money-
changers out of the Temple (John 2:15). He taught his
disciples to 'turn the other cheek' (Luke 6:29).

Yet the society of the Middle Ages was irredeemably
warlike. In the feudal areas of Northern Europe, the
whole social system depended on the maintenance of
a military, or 'knightly', class, a permanent soldiery or
noblemen whose only profession was fighting. In Italy, the
city states were frequently at war – internally, with one
another or with popes and emperors. In Spain, a line was
drawn across the map for some centuries by the presence
of the Muslim invaders. So even if Christians had wanted
to create a peaceful society, it would have been socially
and practically a difficult thing to do.

One way of dealing with this was to idealize the
warfare. The idea of a war between good and evil is very
ancient, and the first 'dualists', the Gnostics, who were
interested in it at the time when Christianity came into
being, presented an ideological challenge, because they
thought in terms of two equal and opposed powers in the
universe, locked in a real struggle for supremacy, in which
the evil might possibly win. Christians had to insist, in
opposition to this widespread view, that there was only
one God and that his opponent was not another deity, but
a fallen angel, a creature who had gone wrong.

In the Christian scheme of explanation, Satan is
merely a fallen angel. He is still a powerful figure, working
systematically and effectively for the possession of human
souls, whom he wishes, in his destructive way, to seduce

from God and to deny any hope of the heaven which is lost to him for ever. For most medieval people, Satan seems to have been a 'personal' threat, rather than an abstraction.

But the battle scenes were attractive. In the Middle Ages, a favourite way of retaining them without slipping into the error of believing that the powers of good and evil in the universe were two deities, was to describe battles between the Virtues and Vices, in which Prudence, Fortitude, Justice and Temperance, in personified form, did battle with their enemies in the form of their opposing vices. The model for this was Prudentius' *Psychomachia* (c. 348–410). It was imitated in the Middle Ages, for example, by Alan of Lille in

A picture of Satan or Lucifer falling from heaven when he sinned, taken from a 'Poor man's Bible' with pictures. From *Codex Palatinus*.

his *Anticlaudianus*. This late 12th-century poem describes an attempt to make a perfect man. The skills available to human knowledge can go only so far, and God has to be asked to provide a soul. However, when the 'perfect man' sets about his task of rescuing the human race, he does it by fighting just such a battle of the virtues and vices.

This kind of literature externalized the inward warfare of which all medieval Christians were encouraged to be aware – that between desires and longings prompted by 'the flesh', and the spiritual aspirations for which God created them.

In the Holy Land, in the 12th century, were 'military' religious orders, whose role was to give protection to

The Christian knight

The 'soldier of Christ', the warrior for good, was not difficult to fit into the Christian scheme of things, even though the reality was that the pervasive fighting of the Middle Ages was far from merely figurative. In the feudal society of Northern Europe in the Middle Ages, the image of the 'soldier of Christ' was important. It enabled laypeople to experience a sense of living for Christ and 'fighting for the good' in their daily lives. It provided an image of great vividness:

In all the city no pagan now appears
Who is not slain or turned to Christian fear.
ANONYMOUS, 'THE SONG OF ROLAND'

There was a good deal of doublethink, in the fact that the penitential system recognized that it was a sin to kill an enemy in battle, even if the battle was in a good cause. The tables of appropriate penances which survive make careful distinctions between the archer who has shot into the enemy line and does not know exactly how many he may have killed or injured, and the foot-soldier or knight who can remember with how many he had hand-to-hand combat, and whether he killed his enemy each time.

'Whenever a man desires anything inordinately, he becomes restless. A proud and avaricious man is never at rest; but a poor and humble man enjoys the riches of peace.'

THOMAS À KEMPIS,
*THE IMITATION OF
CHRIST*, c. 1418

pilgrims, and to provide care and support for Christians on crusade. The Hospitallers and Templars eventually became the subject of criticism and condemnation because some of their actions belied their ideals. Yet, at the beginning of the 12th century, Bernard of Clairvaux could write a 'guided tour' of the Holy Places, drawing spiritual and practical lessons for such hybrid soldier-monks, and telling them how to divide their time between their duties of prayer and their duty to keep their weapons polished.

Just and holy war

It was therefore important for medieval Christians to be able to convince themselves that the war that they were fighting was at least justified. Quite a sophisticated system of identifying a 'just' war grew up. Augustine of Hippo had said a good deal about this, explaining that someone whose property or land has been stolen is entitled to get it back, but that this was different from warfare designed to enlarge one's territory. The underlying principle was that reasonable force could be used to maintain order.

But with the late 11th century came a concept with a new importance – that of 'holy' war, war which God positively wanted his people to fight to restore to Christian control the holy places of the Holy Land. This was war which could not only be regarded as 'justified', and the sins committed in the course of it forgiven, but positively meritorious. God rewarded those who fought it. Guibert of Nogent, in his book *The Acts of God Through the Franks*, explains how to identify 'holy' war. It was not motivated by the desire for fame, money or conquest of lands. Its motive was the protection of liberty, the defence of the state and the protection of the Church. He makes it plain that he himself considered this kind of warfare a valid alternative to being a monk.

This idea was so engaging that, as the 12th century went on, it had to be discouraged by apologists, who did not want everyone to see knighthood as spiritual warfare

Next page: The Christian is often depicted as a knight or warrior, fighting evil. This knight is 'clad in' the virtues and the vices and errors are presented as devils confronting his doves of the peaceful virtues.

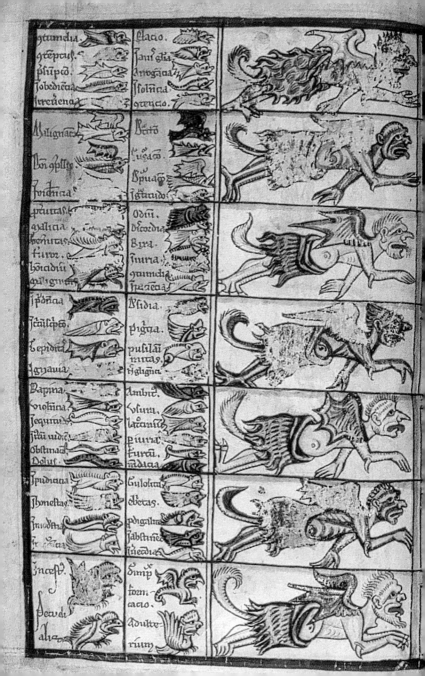

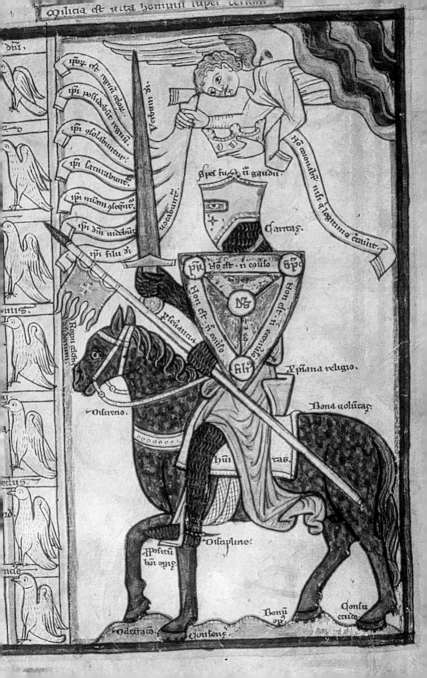

Opposite page:
A medieval
'picture map' of
Jerusalem from
the *Chronicle of
the Crusades* by
Robert the Monk.

*'[He is] the most
distinguished
emperor of the
Roman people,
whose trophies
and valiant
deeds and
stratagems
against the
barbarians the
whole earth
cannot contain.'*

ANNA COMNENA
(1083–c. 1148) ABOUT
HER FATHER, THE
EMPEROR, *ALEXIAD*

to such a degree. It was emphasized that crusading was special. Not all fighting came under the same umbrella.

Muslim literature reflects a similar heightened sense that war could be 'holy'. This period saw the revival of the *jihad*. After the fall of Edessa in 1144 in particular (the first of the crusader states to be regained for Islam after the First Crusade), Muslims increasingly came to see themselves as fighting the Christian polytheist infidels for the glory of God. It eventually became important to the Muslims to recapture Jerusalem itself, to banish the 'worshippers of the cross' from the mosque there. There emerged a 'spiritual *jihad* much greater than the actual battle'.

Crusading

The circumstances in which the Christian West came to engage with 'holy' war were political at the outset. The Turks were invading the Eastern empire. Romanus, the emperor of Byzantium, fought and lost the battle of Manzikert in 1071, and his successor Alexius called on the West to help. This was, in itself, a remarkable proof of how desperate things were. East and West had not been on friendly terms for centuries. The Greeks of the East rather despised the Westerners as barbarians, as is evident from the recorded remarks of Anna Comnena, one of the imperial family. It was as recently as 1054 that the formal Schism of the two Churches had taken place. Yet Alexius wrote to the pope with his plea.

Pope Urban II responded by preaching the crusade at Clermont in 1095. His doing so raised a number of important questions. Here was the primate of the Church, encouraging people to go to war and emphasizing that it was, if not a duty,

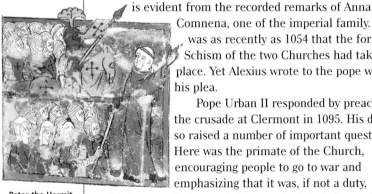

Peter the Hermit
leading the first
crusaders to war.

certainly a meritorious act. He promised that those who went, and either died on the way or stayed the course as far as Jerusalem, would receive full remission of all their undischarged penances (a 'plenary indulgence').

It may be that Urban had an 'ecumenical' purpose. We know that he was keen to mend the breach with the Greek

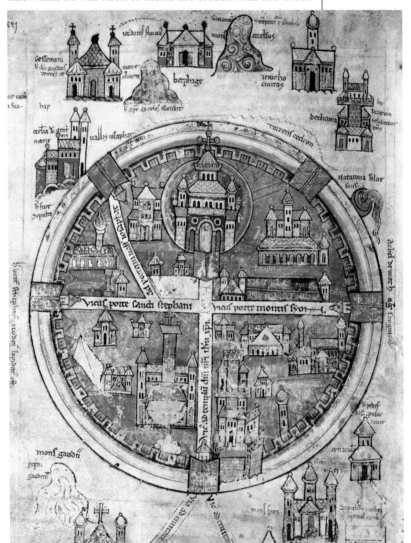

Church. At the Council of Bari in 1098, the matter was raised when Greek Christians were present. Urban called upon Anselm of Canterbury, who had come to him in exile for advice and help in his own dealings with the English king, to stand up at the Council and resolve the difference of opinion about the procession of the Holy Spirit. Anselm tried to do so, asking for a few days to collect his thoughts. Four years later, he published a book giving his opinion, which survives as his *On the Procession of the Holy Spirit*. So Urban's responsiveness to the Byzantine call for help may reflect his wish to reunify Christendom.

In his calling of the crusade, Urban took much the same line as Guibert. The knight who went on crusade was a penitent; he was serving God by bearing arms and he was acting out of sacrificial love, for he may be giving up his life. This was not the mere lending of assistance to a neighbour state in trouble. The 'enemy' were Muslims. The threat was to the holy places. It was a defence of the faith. The language of the Clermont 'decree' spoke of 'going to Jerusalem to liberate the Church of God', and Urban justified the crusade in a letter to the Franks.

Urban saw the Muslim conquest of these places as a contamination, and the task of the crusaders as one of purification.

The crusade, once called, had an immediate attraction for ordinary people, in an age when there were few opportunities for journeys. Itinerant preachers, such as Peter the Hermit, successfully raised armies of peasants. His group, mainly of Germans, was the second to leave. First was Walter Sans Avoir (Walter the Penniless), whose rabble of French peasants set off in 1096, disorganized and plundering as they went through Hungary. The alarmed Byzantines were quick to ship such groups across the Bosphorus into Asia Minor, where they could confront the Turks as they might.

Guibert of Nogent had a fine sense of the sheer scale of the thing. He described how, 'from almost every part of the West', 'innumerable armies' approached. Anselm of

'The barbarians in their frenzy have invaded and ravaged the Churches of God in the Eastern places; worse, they have captured the Holy City of Christ... And sold her and her churches into slavery.'

POPE URBAN II,
*LETTER TO THE
FRANKS*, 1095

Canterbury, who knew and advised Guibert, according to Guibert's autobiography, would not have agreed with him there. Letters survive which were exchanged between Anselm and a young monk anxious for an excuse to leave his monastery and go and fight on crusade.

More senior and organized parties were conducted by leading nobles. Raymond of Toulouse was 60 years old and had fought the Muslims in Spain. Hugh of Vermandois, younger son of King Henry I of France, probably wanted to make a new life outside the unpromising circumstances of his prospective lack of inheritance at home. Godfrey of Bouillon and his younger brother, Baldwin, probably also had designs on lands in the Holy Land. One of the least highly motivated of all, in the kind of terms set out by Guibert of Nogent, seems to have been Robert of Normandy, eldest son of William the Conqueror, who set off with Stephen of Blois and Robert of Flanders.

There were mutual misunderstandings at Constantinople. The emperor exacted an oath of allegiance from Godfrey because he intended to remain in charge of the Western armies if he could. The armies moved off more or less at the same time across Asia Minor in 1097, to encounter in the Turks a formidable and quite unfamiliar style of fighting. The use of Arab horses and light swords, which could be

Fighting the Muslims, a 14th-century French book illumination. Note their short swords which were easier to use effectively on horseback than the crusaders' heavier ones.

used one-handed from horseback to slash an enemy on the gallop, set at a grave disadvantage the slow and cumbersome Western armies. They were experienced in the kind of battle where the opposing sides lined up and charged at one another, and where there was time to stand one's ground and wield a sword with both hands.

Nevertheless, partly with the aid of siege warfare, the crusaders were remarkably successful in this First Crusade, and they were able to establish kingdoms along the Mediterranean seaboard. They built 'crusader castles'.

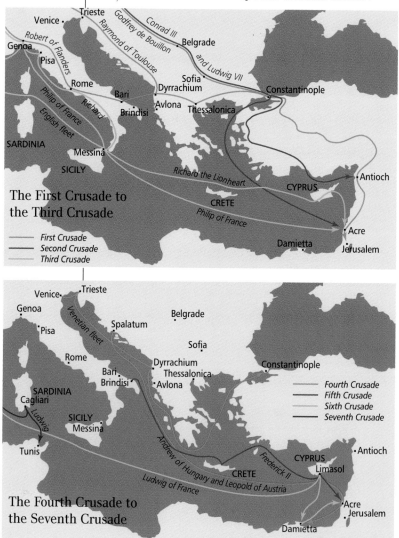

The First Crusade to
the Third Crusade

— First Crusade
— Second Crusade
— Third Crusade

The Fourth Crusade to
the Seventh Crusade

— Fourth Crusade
— Fifth Crusade
— Sixth Crusade
— Seventh Crusade

The success of the First Crusade was acclaimed with a spiritual triumphalism, because it seemed that God must be pleased with the people of the West and what they had done for him. That did not last long. The situation in the Holy Land was inherently unstable even then, though the parties involved were different. The fall of Edessa in 1144 meant that a second crusade had to be called. Bernard of Clairvaux was, at first, reluctant to preach this crusade, because he believed that Christian effort was better directed at making Christendom itself more holy. He was eventually persuaded by Peter the Venerable, the abbot of Cluny who had organized a translation of the Qur'an into Latin so that Christians could have a better idea what Muslims actually believed. Bernard was highly successful in winning people to fight, so much so that supplies of crosses for people to sew on their clothes ran out, and more had to be made by tearing up any cloth to hand. Yet the crusade was an ignominious failure. Instead of recapturing Edessa, the crusaders allowed themselves to be distracted into making a massive attack on Damascus, and thereafter it petered out. Bernard had to explain to

Opposite page: After the triumph of the First Crusade, successive ventures increasingly lost sight of their objectives. By the end of the Fourth Crusade, Jerusalem had been retaken by the Muslims, and Christian Constantinople had been looted as a result of Venetian opportunism.

One of the great 'crusader castles', Krak des Chevaliers.

himself and to others in the West what had gone wrong and why. His explanation was rather like that produced by Augustine after the fall of Rome in 410. God could allow what looked like a Christian enterprise (a Christian empire, a holy war) to fail because he had a far longer-term plan. He was looking to the long-term salvation of his world, and he needed to educate his people, to make them realize how high a standard of goodness was needed for things to work.

A third and a fourth crusade followed, both failures. The Third Crusade (1188–92) was precipitated by the fall

Pilgrimage

Talk of pilgrimage may not seem to have a natural place in a chapter on holy war, but the pilgrimage context was important to the way in which the crusaders saw what they were doing. Pilgrimage to the holy places had been becoming popular during the 11th century. There was an understandable conflation in people's minds between the journey of pilgrimage, the journey which was crusade and the journey which was a person's metaphorical travelling through life. Jerusalem was both 'heavenly' and 'earthly', and because it was so far away, it may not always have been clear to those who set out to go there that they were not really travelling directly to heaven. Many different Latin words to do with travelling were used, and almost all of them could apply equally well to literal or spiritual 'travelling' of the body or the soul.

The bringing together of the physical and the supernatural world in this way is visible in much earlier writing. Avitus, Bishop of Vienne (495–525) says, 'there is a place, far on the eastern side of the world' where winter and summer do not follow one another in succession. Gregory the Great, at the end of the sixth century, spoke of the fields where the sheep of Christ the shepherd fed, spending eternity in the presence of God and contemplating eternally he who was their spiritual food.

To be able to think of oneself as going to this place by the simple expedient of setting off on an expedition was a powerful idea. It was linked with the ancient Platonic and Christian idea that all creation is on a journey back to God. The 'region' close to God is the 'region of likeness'. Sinful humans have wandered off into the 'region of unlikeness' (*regio dissimilitudinis*), and their life's task is to return to God.

of Jerusalem to the Muslims under Saladin. It drew in reigning monarchs to lead it: Frederick Barbarossa, the emperor of Germany; Philip Augustus, king of France; and King Henry II of England. The resulting political rivalries made the failure of the crusade almost inevitable.

The Fourth Crusade (1204), in particular, displayed a crude commercialism on the part of the Venetians, who required the crusaders to sack Constantinople first, in return for the use of ships for transport. The sight, in 1204, of Western Christians running about the streets of the great city, which was the capital of the Christian East, sacking, pillaging and raping was the ultimate betrayal of the ideal of the crusade as a holy war, although the crusading movement lasted into the 13th century, in a desultory way..

A portrait, probably of Saladin.

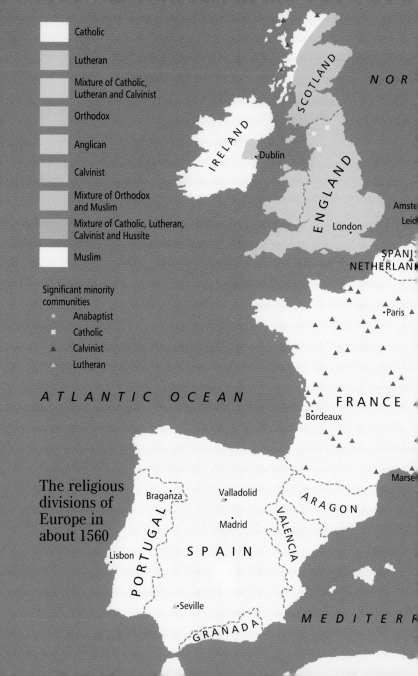

Legend:

- Catholic
- Lutheran
- Mixture of Catholic, Lutheran and Calvinist
- Orthodox
- Anglican
- Calvinist
- Mixture of Orthodox and Muslim
- Mixture of Catholic, Lutheran, Calvinist and Hussite
- Muslim

Significant minority communities
- ● Anabaptist
- ▪ Catholic
- ▲ Calvinist
- ▲ Lutheran

The religious divisions of Europe in about 1560

ATLANTIC OCEAN

N O R

SCOTLAND

IRELAND

·Dublin

ENGLAND

London

Amste
Leid

SPANI
NETHERLAN

·Paris

FRANCE

Bordeaux

Marse

PORTUGAL

Braganza

Valladolid

Madrid

ARAGON

VALENCIA

SPAIN

Lisbon

·Seville

GRANADA

M E D I T E R R A

C H A P T E R   1 0

Tradition and Continuity: the Road to Reformation

S everal things happened in the West in the 15th and 16th centuries to change the medieval scene so irrevocably that the period which followed could begin to be spoken of as the 'modern world'. As so often, the dividing lines separating what now look to us like distinct 'periods' were different in the Eastern half of Christendom. A detailed picture of this is available in *Faith in the Byzantine World*, another title in this series.

Another book in this series, *Luther and His World*, describes Luther's significant role in making people think differently and in opening up the lasting divisions in the Christian Church which can still be seen today in the numerous 'denominations', with their separate church buildings and their separated congregations. The ecumenical movement of the second half of the 20th century did a good deal to mend these divisions, but it has not yet succeeded in putting the Western Churches back where they were in 1400, or in bringing together the East and West, which parted in 1054. It is probably still true that there is fundamentally one 'faith', but it is obvious that there is not, in any visible sense, one Church.

Renaissance

Alongside the changes in the Church ran an immense change of expectations among scholars, which was able to move with unprecedented speed because of the invention of printing. Printed books began to appear before the end of the 15th century, and during the course of the 16th century, printed versions were produced of a good proportion of the main works of the Middle Ages.

An early printer at work. The press can be seen, and on the right the 'typesetter' assembling the letters in a frame ready to print copies of the book he is working from.

Medieval scholars invented the universities, and the universities, too, began to change, with 'alternative syllabuses'. The medieval method of study had gradually evolved into a system which is often labelled 'scholasticism'. There was a heavy burden of 'system', derived from the formal study of logic. Aristotle remained the basis but, in the medieval centuries, a 'new logic' was added. This built on Aristotle and dealt in a much more subtle and sophisticated way with the way in which language works. Given a problem, a teacher would divide it up for his students, and they would look at each part of it in order. This could have the effect of reducing all issues to the same level. It made it difficult to be inventive or to find new ways of approaching the framing and answering of questions.

Two Renaissance men

One of the first scholars to bring together the new 'Greek' learning and the transformation of the approach to the study

of the Christian faith was Erasmus. He enjoyed the civilized wit of the Renaissance, which is reflected in his writings – for example, in *In Praise of Folly*, to which he gave a Greek title. An English contemporary and friend was Thomas More – lawyer, parliamentarian and scholar – who kept open house in London for Erasmus and his circle. More also wrote, notably, the famous *Utopia*, in which he imagines an ideal state and its drawbacks. These 'Renaissance men' were not always sympathetic to the Reform which was being called for in the Church. More was a staunch defender of the medieval Church while King Henry VIII was moving towards the breach with Rome, and he suffered for it politically. More was beheaded for treason in 1535 because he opposed the king's divorce. He wrote a *Response to Luther*: 'When I began to read – good God, what an ocean of nonsense, what a bottomless pit of madness presented itself.'

Erasmus of
Rotterdam
(c. 1466–1536)
by Hans Holbein
the Younger.

Lorenzo Valla, in the late 15th century, began to point to drawbacks in the scholastic method. Peter Ramus, in the 16th century, took Aristotle and the 'new logic' by the scruff of the neck, and reduced it all to a simple introductory course. He did not do it very well, but his work was welcomed by students because this marked the end of the dominance of the medieval pattern of study.

At the same time, there was a reawakening ('Renaissance') of enthusiasm for the classics, not only for the Roman authors, such as Cicero, Livy, Horace and Seneca, who had been available all through the Middle Ages, but also the Greek ones. They were now becoming accessible to more readers because students were beginning to learn Greek. This trend was not separate from the moves which were leading to the Reformation. Melanchthon was a leading 'Renaissance' scholar and a close friend of Luther, working with him in running the University of Wittenberg.

The head of
Plato. Roman
marble bust
from Smyrna.

The 'double life' of scholars who could write on secular themes and, at the same time, make a serious mark as theologians or writers on religious subjects was in evidence throughout the 16th century. John Donne, who became Dean of St Paul's, was able to write in jest, but not without seriousness, about holy things and theological ideas in a love poem, 'Air and Angels'.

So in a voice, so in a shapeless flame
Angels affect us oft and worshipp'd be...
And therefore what thou wert, and who,
I bid love ask, and now
That is assume thy body I allow,
And fix itself in thy lip, eye, and brow.

JOHN DONNE (1571/2–1631), 'AIR AND ANGELS'

Back to the sources
The last great medieval development in the study of the Bible, too, was the call to get back to the sources (*ad fontes*). Here, the reawakening of interest in the

'biblical languages' of Greek and Hebrew was important. In the 12th century, a few scholars, such as Andrew of St Victor, asked the advice of Jews who spoke Hebrew when they were unsure of how they should 'read' a passage in the Old Testament. However, this does not seem to have led to serious attempts to learn the language for themselves. The late Middle Ages saw the founding of universities which specialized in teaching the three 'biblical languages' of Greek, Hebrew and Latin. Reuchlin (1455–1522), a German humanist, was one of the first individuals to tackle instruction in Hebrew systematically, by providing textbooks to help students to learn it.

In the same period, others – notably, perhaps, Erasmus of Rotterdam – were beginning to work seriously on the Greek. (Erasmus confessed that he could not manage to learn both languages at once.) Erasmus published a Greek New Testament in 1516, and made a fresh version of the Latin Vulgate to go with it. His notes on the New Testament survive – a personal, witty, satirical commentary on the problems he faced. He was working on his *In Praise of Folly* at about the same time, and in something of the same comico-serious spirit. He was a humanist, and therefore conscious of classical comparisons and allusions. Considering the possible translations of the beginning of Matthew's Gospel, he observed that 'sometimes Homer used this word in the Odyssey, but that Matthew means something quite new when he uses it'. His intention was not to overturn the Vulgate as the Bible of the Western Church, but he could not help noticing its flaws. He is critical, but he 'pretends' that he cannot really believe that the Vulgate was the work of the great Jerome; perhaps the translator sometimes 'nodded off'? Erasmus, still learning Greek, nevertheless thought that he could usefully use the Greek New Testament in making his own Latin rendering.

One of the striking results of this kind of work was that it enabled scholars to look at the text in a new way and ask fresh questions. A quite different sort of early printed Bible began to appear, known as the Polyglot, because it set the text in various languages side by side for comparison.

Change in the Church

The Reformation idea of 'justification by faith' was largely a creation of Martin Luther. He had been disturbed by the growing elaborateness of the Church's expectations at the end of the Middle Ages, the insistence that no one could get to heaven without the good offices of the Church and its sacraments. He brought about an immense 'shake-up', by arguing passionately that God was interested only in the individual's personal faith, and that this was what 'justified' people in God's eyes. No one could get to heaven merely by doing good works, or through the penitential system of 'making up' for wrongdoing.

A drawing of Martin Luther (1483–1546) by his friend Melanchthon.

Luther's proposition undermined much of the structure we have been looking at in this book, because it threw into question what the Church was for and whether the faithful needed its 'official' help to be saved. The visible Church, with all its imperfections and corruptions, was actively contrasted in the 16th century with the spiritual and invisible Church.

Some reformers (the 'Congregation-alists') argued that the Church as a whole was invisible, but that it had visible 'outcrops' in the form of local congregations. Much emphasis was placed on the self-government of these 'gathered churches', in order to weaken the stranglehold of the centralized and monarchical structure which had emerged in the Church in the West as a result of the mounting claims of the papacy to 'plenitude of power'.

This led other reformers to go back to the New Testament and to point to the apparent lack of authority there for the threefold system of ministry which was, by now, fixed in the structure and governance of the Church. Some of them (the 'Presbyterians') began to avoid the terminology of 'bishop' and 'priest', in favour of 'presbyter'.

A serious area of disquiet in the Reformation West concerned the traditional powers of priests. The trend away from the ministry of the word was being reversed by the new concentration on the study of the Bible. The cry was now *sola scriptura* ('scripture alone'). That left the ministry of the sacraments. There, the late-medieval tendency had been to treat the 'saying of the Mass' as something a priest alone could do, and not as an action in which all the worshipping community should be involved. We saw in an earlier chapter how the development in the 11th and 12th centuries of the doctrine of transubstantiation had led to a belief that, when an ordained priest said Jesus' words, 'This is my body' and 'This is my blood', the bread and wine of the eucharist, or holy communion, turned literally into the body and blood of Christ. So, the 'power' to say Mass became enormous, with the priests, some said, 'adding to' the sacrifice Christ himself made on the cross.

The question, 'What is a bishop for?' became sharper than usual in the second quarter of the 16th century, as dispute fastened on the theology of ministry and other aspects of theology which were turning out to be Church-

A statue of
Thomas Aquinas
(c. 1226–1274)
in La Quercia.

dividing. In 1559, most dioceses were without a bishop, and it was unclear whether there would be any bishops in the future.

In England, the bishops were historically 'the king's men' as well as the Church's. The old battles of the Investiture Contest loomed again, with Archbishop William Wareham defending himself in 1532 against the charge that he had consecrated the Bishop of St Asaph in 1518 before the king had confirmed the grant of 'temporalities'. He made the striking claim that 'a man is not made bishop by consecration, but is pronounced so at Rome in Consistory'. The consecration gave him the 'rights of his order', but not its jurisdiction. This kind of thing was central to the discussion of whether the king could not take over part of the making of a bishop, which had hitherto fallen to Rome.

These structural questions about the exercise (or abuse) of power in the Church were enough to open up those 'divides' which have persisted so stubbornly. There were individuals in addition to Luther (notably, John Calvin and Huldrych Zwingli) who won personal support as leaders of the questioning, and as founders of new churches or communities of believers.

Out on the edges were the charismatics again. The Anabaptists argued that there was no need for the sacraments, not even for baptism, nor for any ordained ministry. The people of God needed nothing more than the Bible and the help of the Holy Spirit.

Over against these changes, and replying vigorously to the awkward questions which were being raised, stood the continuing medieval Church. The Council of Trent, in the middle of the 16th century, took stock of it all and dug its heels in. The old literature and practice continued there, despite the Reformation and the Renaissance. Indeed, it was in the 16th century that the 13th-century *Summa Theologiae* of Thomas Aquinas finally became established as a standard authority for teaching theology.

Imaginative and risk-taking writing of great beauty was still possible in what was by no means a defeated Church.

'We have learned from the grammarians that the words "This is my body" cannot correctly be turned into "In this bread the body of Christ is eaten."'

HULDRYCH ZWINGLI
(1484–1531)

St John of the Cross wrote of Christ as a shepherd boy
whose beloved (the soul as the bride of Christ) spurned him.

Time passed: on a season he sprang from the ground,
  Swarned a tall tree and arms balancing wide
Beautifully grappled the tree till he died
  Of the love in his heart like a ruinous wound.

ST JOHN OF THE CROSS (1542–91)

Come ye to judgement.
  For now is set the high justice,
And the day of doom...
  when God shall examine, beware!
The truth alone he will hear
  And send you to heaven or hell.

ANONYMOUS, *THE ENGLISH PASSION PLAY*

The culture of the medieval world was steeped in the
expectations and assumptions of the Christian faith to a
degree which is not easy for the modern reader to enter into.

The last things

Still generally accepted without question in the 16th century
was the habit of looking beyond this world to a better one,
which the medieval picture of the cosmos had encouraged.
This was reflected in medieval historical writing and in drama,
as well as in theological and spiritual writings. Medieval
historians often began with the creation of the world and
went on to the present day, as though it were all one
historical sequence. This gave their tales a great dignity and
scale, which was important when historians were really chiefly
interested in glorifying the small local subject of their story, or
creating a 'myth' about their own people. Bede may have
been doing that when he wrote *The Ecclesiastical History of
the English People*. Whatever his local 'political' motives, he
took it for granted that the proper place for human history
was 'in the context of eternity' (*sub specie eternitatis*).

Even taking East (the Greek Church) and West (the Roman Church) together, today's Christian believer is conscious of being in a cultural 'minority'. Those of other faiths are living openly, side-by-side, in the same communities. Those who are Christians are not always easily identifiable as such to colleagues and acquaintances. There are remnants of the cultural dominance of Christianity in the social expectations of the modern West, but the West itself is no longer uncontroversially 'dominant'. Nor should it be.

From the 16th century, the 'known world' grew bigger. Civilizations hitherto not in contact with the Christian West were 'discovered' (the American continent), became more active trading partners (parts of the East) or the fields of colonization (Africa). There was a form of 'globalization' which was slower and more ponderous than is possible through modern electronic communication. Yet it nonetheless transformed the 'world' of the Middle Ages into something bigger and more diverse.

Today, the great 'test' is the capacity of the Christian religion to flourish in the immense variety of cultural contexts in which it is now found. We have watched it become 'inculturated' in a thousand years of the medieval period. Its modern integration is another story.

Chronology

46–62: The apostle Paul goes on his missionary journeys, and new local churches multiply.

By fourth century: New Testament written, the Christian Bible created and approved by the Church. Donatism causing schism in north Africa.

325: Council of Nicea condemns heresy of Arius and creates the Nicene Creed; First Ecumenical Council.

337: Death of Constantine the Great, the first Christian emperor.

354–430: Augustine of Hippo.

381: Council of Constantinople confirms Nicene Creed; Second Ecumenical Council.

Fifth century: Conversion of Ireland by St Patrick.

431: Council of Ephesus, Third Ecumenical Council.

c. 480–c. 550: Benedict of Nursia, founder of the Benedictine Order of monks.

451: Council of Chalcedon, results in separation of the non-Chalcedonian Churches of the East, Fourth Ecumenical Council.

553: Council of Constantinople, Fifth Ecumenical Council.

596: Conversion of England by Augustine of Canterbury, sent by Pope Gregory the Great.

c. 672–735: The Venerable Bede.

787: Council of Nicea seeks to end the iconoclast controversy and restore icons.

962: First monastery founded on Mount Athos.

1033–1109: Anselm of Bec and Canterbury.

1054: Schism between Greek and Roman Churches over papal primacy and the addition of the *filioque* clause to the Nicene Creed.

1090–1153: Bernard of Clairvaux, great Cistercian leader.

1096: First Crusade.

12th century: Popular anti-establishment and dualist heresies flourish in France and northern Spain.

1204: Fourth Crusade ends the main crusading period.

1215: Fourth Lateran Council, creates more formal requirements in the penitential system.

13th century: Franciscan and Dominican Orders of friars flourish and begin to take over the academic life of the new universities.

1274: Thomas Aquinas dies.

1309–77: Papacy in exile at Avignon.

1378–1417: Great Schism of the papacy in the West.

1384: John Wyclif dies.

1414–18: Council of Constance condemns Wyclif and Jan Hus for heresy.

1438–45: Council of Florence, attempts to mend the Schism of 1054.

1483: Martin Luther born.

Suggestions for Further Reading

The series *Classics of Western Spirituality* includes translations of the works of many medieval authors, from both the East and the West. Penguin's *Penguin Classics* and Oxford University Press's *World Classics* are also useful series in which to find examples of medieval writing. A few texts are given below in the 'Further Reading' lists for individual chapters, from which the reader may begin to get the 'flavour' of the Christian writing of the Middle Ages. But there is no better way to enter the medieval world of thought than to read as widely as possible in the original writings.

Chapter 1: The World Through Medieval Eyes

Augustine of Hippo, *Confessions*, tr. Henry Chadwick, *World Classics*, Oxford: Oxford University Press, 1991.

A.D. Nock, *Conversion*, Oxford: Oxford University Press, 1933.

Aristeides Papadakis and John Meyendorff, *The Christian East and the Rise of the Papacy*, New York: St Vladimir, 1994.

William C. Placker, *Theology: From its Beginnings to the Eve of the Reformation*, Philadelphia: Westminster Press, 1998.

R.W. Southern, *Western Society and the Church in the Middle Ages*, Harmondsworth: Penguin, 1970, reprinted 1990.

John A.F. Thompson, *The Western Church in the Middle Ages*, Oxford: Arnold and Oxford University Press, 1998.

Chapter 2: What Did Medieval Christians Believe?

Peter Abelard, *Ethical Writings*, tr. Paul Vincent Spade, Indianapolis/Cambridge: Hackett, 1995.

Thomas Aquinas, *Selected Philosophical Writings*, tr. T. McDermott, *World Classics*, Oxford: Oxford University Press, 1993.

Bede, *A Biblical Miscellany*, tr. W. Trent Foley and Arthur G. Holden, Liverpool: Liverpool University Press, 1999.

Henry Chadwick, *The Early Church*, Harmondsworth: Penguin, 1967.

J.M. Rist, *Plotinus: The Road to Reality*, Cambridge: Cambridge Uinversity Press, 1967.

Maxwell Staniforth and Andrew Louth (tr.), *Early Christian Writings: The Apostolic Fathers*, *Penguin Classics*, Harmondsworth: Penguin, 1987.

Chapter 3: Bible Study

H. de Lubac, *Medieval Exegesis* (two volumes), tr. E.M. Macierowski, Paris: Eerdmans and T. and T. Clark, 1998–2000.

G.R. Evans, *The Language and Logic of the Bible* (two volumes), Cambridge: Cambridge University Press, 1984, 1985.

M. Simonetti, *Biblical Interpretation in the Early Church*, tr. J.A. Hughes, Edinburgh: T and T. Clark, 1994.

Beryl Smalley, *The Study of the Bible in the Middle Ages* (third edition), Oxford: Oxford University Press, 1983.

Chapter 4: Defining the Church

Tr. R. Davis, *The Book of Pontiffs (Liber Pontificalis): Ancient Biographies of the First Ninety Roman Bishops* (second edition), Liverpool: Liverpool University Press, 2000.

Eamon Duffy, *The Stripping of the Altars*, Yale: Yale University Press, 1992.

Norman P. Tanner, *Councils of the Church: a Short History*, London: Heider, 2001.

T.F. Tentler, *Sin and Confession on the Eve of the Reformation*, Princeton: Princeton University Press, 1977.

Chapter 5: Laypeople

Eamon Duffy, *The Stripping of the Altars*, Yale: Yale University Press, 1992.

Anne Hudson, *The Premature Reformation*, Oxford; Oxford University Press, 1987.

Julian of Norwich, *Showings*, tr. Edmund Colledge and James Walsh, *Classics of Western Spirituality*, New York: Paulist Press, 1978.

Chapter 6: Politics and the Church

Brian Tierney, *The Crisis of Church and State, 1050–1300*, New York: Spectrum, 1964.

Brian Tierney, *The Origins of Papal Infallibility, 1150–1350*, Leiden: Brill, 1972.

Walter Ullman, *The Origins of the Great Schism*, Connecticut: Hamden, 1972.

Michael Wilks, *The Problem of Sovereignty in the Later Middle Ages*, Cambridge: Cambridge University Press, 1963.

Chapter 7: The Rebels

R. Cross, *Duns Scotus*, Oxford: Oxford University Press, 1999.

Master Eckhardt, *Selected Writings*, tr. Oliver Davies, Harmondsworth: Penguin, 1994.

Anne Hudson, *The Premature Reformation*, Oxford: Oxford University Press, 1988.

Bernard McGinn (tr.), *Apocalyptic Spirituality*, Classics of Western Spirituality, London: SPCK, 1980.

Bernard McGinn, *Visions of the End: Apocalyptic Traditions in the Middle Ages*, New York: Columbia, 2000.

Michael Wilks, *Wyclif, Political Ideas and Practice*, Oxford: Oxbow, 2000.

Chapter 8: Monks, Saints and Christian Examples

Mark Atherton (tr.), *Hildegard of Bingen: Selected Writings*, Penguin Classics, Harmondsworth: Penguin, 2001.

Peter Brown, *The Cult of the Saints*, Chicago: University of Chicago Press, 1981.

C.H. Lawrence, *Medieval Monasticism* (third edition), London: Pearson Education, 2001.

Fiona Maddocks, *Hildegard of Bingen: A Woman of Her Age*, London: Hodder Headline, 2001.

P. Matarasso (tr.), *The Cistercian World – Monastic Writings of the Twelfth Century*, Harmondsworth: Penguin, 1993.

Gregory Palamas, *Triads*, tr. J. Meyendorff and Nicholas Gendle, *Classics of Western Spirituality*, London: SPCK, 1983.

Chapter 9: Holy War

W.B. Bartlett, *God Wills It*, Stroud: Alan Sutton, 1999.

Guibert de Nogent, *Gesta dei per Francos*, tr. R. Levine, Woodbridge: Boydell, 1997.

J. Riley-Smith, *The First Crusade*, Cambridge: Cambridge University Press, 1997.

Chapter 10: Tradition and Continuity: the Road to Reformation

Gerald Brady (ed.), *Documents of the English Reformation*, Cambridge: James Clarke, 1994.

E. Cameron, *The European Reformation*, Oxford: Oxford University Press, 1991.

Owen Chadwick, *The Reformation*, Harmondsworth: Penguin, 1964.

Alister E. McGrath, *Reformation Thought: An Introduction* (third edition), Oxford: Blackwell, 2000.

Index

Picture and Text Acknowledgments

Pictures

Picture research by Zooid Pictures Limited.

AKG London: pp. 12 (Cameraphoto), 15, 22 (Erich Lessing), 31 (Orsi Battaglini), 38 (Stefan Diller), 43 (British Library), 52, 53, 55, 59 (Stefan Diller), 65 (British Library), 66–67, 68, 73 (Erich Lessing), 76, 77, 80–81, 86 (British Library), 96, 106–107, 114–15, 124–25 (Jean-François Amelot), 129, 132–33 (British Library), 134 (British Library), 137, 139 (Tarek Camoisson), 146 (Erich Lessing), 147 (Erich Lessing).

Art Archive: pp. 69 (Eileen Tweedy/Victoria and Albert Museum, London), 94 (Biblioteca Nazionale Palermo/Dagli Orti).

Bridgeman Art Library: p. 89 (Bibliothèque Nationale, Paris, France).

Corbis UK Ltd: pp. 1 (Araldo de Luca), 2–3 (Elio Ciol), 4–5 (Archivo Iconografico, S.A.), 6–7 (Paul Almasy), 16 (WildCountry), 19 (Archivo Iconografico, S.A.), 25 (David Lees), 34 (Chris Hellier), 37 (Vanni Archive), 44 (Leonard de Selva), 50 (Araldo de Luca), 62 (top, Patrick Ward), 62 (bottom, Archivo Iconografico, S.A.), 82 (Bill Ross), 83 (Francesco Venturi/Kea Publishing Services Ltd), 85 (Archivo Iconografico, S.A.), 97 (Archivo Iconografico, S.A.), 100 (both, Bettmann), 103 (David Lees), 111 (Yann Arthus-Bertrand), 118–19 (Paul Almasy), 121 (National Gallery Collection; by kind permission of the Trustees of the National Gallery, London), 135 (Gianni Dagli Orti), 141 (Bettmann), 145 (Bettmann), 149 (James L. Amos), 150 (Sandro Vannini).

Heritage Image Partnership: p. 117 (British Library).

Mary Evans Picture Library: p. 47.

Derek West: maps on pp. 138, 142–43.

Text

Lion Publishing

Commissioning editor: Morag Reeve

Project editor: Jenni Dutton

Insides designer: Nicholas Rous

Jacket designer: Jonathan Roberts

Production controller: Charles Wallis